Embracing Death:
A New Look
at Grief, Gratitude and God

By Terri Daniel

with
Danny Mandell

WORKSHOP EDITION

© 2010

Linda —
Many thanks
+ blessings!

July 2012

Embracing Death:
A New Look
at Grief, Gratitude and God

By Terri Daniel
With
Danny Mandell

Workshop Edition
© 2010

**This is the *workshop edition* of this book,
and is not intended for mass distribution**

The mass distribution edition
(ISBN: 978-1-84694-360-7)
is published by O-Books
and can be ordered from:

National Book Network (NBN)
custserv@nbnbooks.com
800 462 6420
www.nbnbooks.com

**To Danny
and his Heavenly Homeboys**

With eternal gratitude
to my beloved guides and guardians

Acknowledgments

Immense gratitude and love to those who have assisted, inspired and supported me in the creation of this book:

Anna Bonas, DC LAC OMD
Carolyn Weislogel
Chrystal Wadsworth
Cynthia Morrow-Hattal, Ph.D
Danika Campfield
David Staume
Diane Gobel, MSCC, CCHt
George Bonano, Ph.D
George Bonano, Ph.D.
Joellyn St. Pierre, D. Div.
John Hunt and O Books
Judy Gibson
Ken Stoller, MD
Krista Goering
Lindsay Roberts
Lori Justice-Shocket
Lorilee Friedland
Marietta Roby
Marilyn Rose
Mukesh Chaturvedi
Niel Shocket, MD
Odani Keiko
Rebecca Covington
Robin Clark
Sue and Boyd Coxen
Suzy Ward
The Danny Dialogs

Special thanks to Pamela Jo Hunter for cover design

CONTENTS

Introduction

"Is it true there is a cure for all illness?
Only if you are wise enough to see death as a cure."

Emmanuel's Book

As an afterlife awareness educator and mother of a child who died at age 16 after a lengthy illness, I am fiercely committed to the idea of conscious dying and conscious grieving. By understanding that death is neither an enemy nor an ending, the process of grieving the death of a loved one becomes a journey of awakening for the person who has died *and* for those who remain on earth.

I've spent a lifetime studying metaphysics and spirituality, and I believe unequivocally that there are no "good" or "bad" experiences; only the soul's constant craving for growth and expansion. In this view, illness and death are not experiences to be avoided, but to be embraced with gratitude for the shifting of perceptions and gifts of growth they provide. In a state of gratitude at this level, we accept every experience with love, because we recognize it as one of our soul's creations. Even something as painful as the death of a child can be seen as part of a flawless pattern of perfection that moves the family and the entire soul group forward in unexpected ways.

When my son Danny was diagnosed with a life-threatening illness at age 10, friends and family asked, "Does this change your unconventional spiritual views? Does it make you want to go back to traditional notions of God, afterlife and religion?"

This might have been a good question for someone who'd taken only a few tentative steps outside the religious box during her lifetime, but for me, the question was preposterous. The stunning news that my son would only live a few more years actually confirmed what I'd intuitively known since I was a teenager... there are pre-birth agreements between souls. Reincarnation is real. There's a reason for everything. And we create our own experiences on earth with the assistance of non-physical guides and helpers.

Metaphysical thinking was nothing new to me. In 1966 when I was 13 years old, I found a collection of books about world religions on my father's bookshelf, and read them all. He also had a copy of Carl Jung's *Man and his Symbols,* and I remember reading it on the bus on the way to and from junior high school. The following year, a Krishna Consciousness congregation moved into an old church in my neighborhood and I attended their Sunday feasts and listened to lectures by their teacher, Swami Bhaktivedanta. When I was 16, my liberal, free-thinking high school English teacher taught the first five books of the Bible as *literature,* and from there, fueled by intense curiosity, I went on to read the rest of it (my family was not religious at all, and the high school class was my first exposure to this material). By the time I was 19 I'd read the Tibetan Book of the Dead, Ruth Montgomery and Edgar Cayce. These teachings resonated with me as absolute truth back then, and over the years, supported by further study and practice, these truths were confirmed again and again. So when Danny was diagnosed, I knew instantly that his soul had a plan of its own. And it was my intention to honor *his* intention.

Let's go back for a moment to those traditional notions of God, afterlife and religion. Had I perceived this situation through that lens, I might have been gripped with fear and helplessness, too puny and unworthy to comprehend the mysterious workings of an all-powerful God who randomly dispenses good or bad luck, sorrow or joy, wealth or poverty in life, and reward or punishment in death. By contrast, a more *self-empowered* spirituality says that we are not at the mercy of a humanoid God who is separate from us, but are equal parts of a collective energy that IS God, an energy with which we work as co-creators. This work is done "on earth as it is in Heaven," as our souls continually seek experience in and out of the body. The growth work we do during our earthly incarnations carries over to the Other Side, where we evaluate and create new and effective situations to bring forth the ideal experiences to fuel our continued exploration. In this way there can be no tragedies, no here and there, no them and us, and no death.

Over the years, my passion for examining death from the perspective of both the dying and the grieving led me to an interesting mix of studies and practices drawn from all the usual sources and many of the not-so-usual ones. One of those sources is The Anamcara Project, a unique spiritual education program created by Richard and Mary Groves. Their Sacred Art of Living and Dying seminars have attracted more than 10,000 students from a wide range of healing professions and the general public, including educators, clergy, hospice workers, physicians and metaphysicians. I was drawn to the program when I first heard the term, "spiritual midwife," referring to someone who helps the dying make their transitions from this world to the next. Because the word "midwife" so perfectly described the role I played in Danny's death, I sought out the Anamcara Project, and it became an important part of not only my work as a hospice volunteer, but my personal growth path as well.

One of the things I learned in the Anamcara training is that in the early hospices it was understood that death is not the opposite of life, but the opposite of *birth,* or in a sense, *the same as* birth. In many of these hospices it was common to see women giving birth on one side of the room while people were dying on the other side, all guided by midwives, while minstrels strolled around playing soothing music. Death may not be the opposite of life, but it is certainly a part of life, and there are many social and religious traditions that recognize and honor death as the sacred, intimate journey that it is.

But sadly, modern America has created a culture of denial around death, and hospice care is still not generally understood or accepted. In ancient times the word "hospice" literally meant 'hospitality,' a process of assisting travelers with their journeys, including the journeys of birth and death. In those times we lived closer to the land; we saw people and animals die all the time, and there was very little about it that was terrible or frightening. The terror came with religious doctrine and the concept of evil and punishment, which embedded the fear of death into our thinking.

One of the greatest losses to our society over the last few generations is the sacred process of caring for our dead at home. Before the industrial revolution, when grandmother was dying, she was surrounded by her family, including young children, and after death her body was cleaned, dressed and laid out on a table for viewing by friends and family. The body was then buried in a family graveyard on the family acreage. It was a natural and expected passage, and there is now a growing movement in the U.S. to return to these practices in the hope of bringing death back into light and out of the dark place where it's been relegated by fear, repression and religious dogma. Danny had a beautiful death at home, with his beloved dog and his family by his side. I'd learned from the home death movement that a body can stay at home much longer than modern practices dictate, and we kept Danny's body with us for five hours before calling the mortuary. It gave us a chance to gently and consciously release his physical presence, and to honor the sacred vessel that had done such a worthy job of housing his soul.

A "good death" should be as fearless as possible, and one way to lessen that fear is to seek alternative views that honor our intuitive knowledge, our non-physical senses and our inner gifts while eliminating the notion of Divine punishment. Embracing death with boundless leaps of faith can shift the experience of life-threatening illness or trauma from terrifying to transcendent. An understanding of our own divinity and the perfect journey of our souls, supported by guides, angels and loved ones who have passed before us, helps us understand death as simply a journey to another room, where life continues in a different form and all deaths are pathways to healing.

Author's Note

I am not a religious scholar, nor do I claim to be part of an elite illuminati whose mission is to dole out Divine secrets to humanity. I don't even have a college degree (though I'm working on one now, in the my late 50s), and my credentials for the work I do aren't verifiable by traditional methods. I'm simply someone who receives channeled information from beings in the non-physical realms, and I happen to have a knack for writing, which is apparently why they chose me for this work. I share what I am given. I'm a scribe, nothing more.

I primarily channel one being who has been close to me for many lifetimes. He most recently incarnated as my adopted son Danny, and lived on earth as my only child and my constant companion for 16 years. During his brief stay here, he was afflicted with a rare degenerative disorder that rendered him severely disabled for the last eight years of his life. He died in 2006 and began speaking to me telepathically immediately after his passing. Together we wrote a book called *A Swan in Heaven,* which recounted the dialogs we shared between dimensions. Those dialogs continue to this day, and are the foundation of my work as an author and afterlife awareness educator.

Danny has, over the past few years, introduced me to other beings who are his friends and teachers in the higher planes of consciousness, which he calls *Heaven,* and now we all work together as a consortium. I provide the human capabilities of speaking and writing while Danny and his "Heavenly homeboys" (as he sometimes calls them) gives me a steady stream of information about birth, death and the journey of the soul. With the help of this eager team of invisible helpers, I write books, conduct workshops and act as a metaphysical grief guidance facilitator for the bereaved.

Most of the writing in this book is in my own human voice, even though I'm relaying information that's being transmitted to me by Danny and his teaching team. But sometimes their words and concepts are so achingly beautiful, richly detailed and full of Divine love that I've simply inserted their messages, word-for-word as they were given (you'll recognize when they chime in because the text appears in a different format). When I write in the narrative, my earthly ego nature comes through, because as a human, I can be prone to judgment, anger, sarcasm and other non-Heavenly attributes. But when my guides are speaking, their loving voices are unmistakably gentle and unbiased. As their mouthpiece on earth, it's humbling for me to move between our worlds.

In the early days of my channeled writing I could clearly feel the difference between my voice and theirs. It was usually signaled by a subtle energy shift and a very obvious change in writing "voice." As time went on however, it became difficult to tell if it was them speaking or me, because we had merged into a sort of composite in which their thoughts and mine occur simultaneously. The more I blended with them, the more I began to see the interconnectedness of everything in the universe, and this view fills me with gratitude every hour of every day.

I embrace and believe these messages fully and fearlessly, and I live my life as if they are indisputably true. While I experience the same trials and traumas as any other human -- loss, grief, relationship struggles, health issues and financial hardships -- I view these experiences with a different perspective. Because I've learned that we have endless opportunities to create our experiences and that life doesn't end with the expiration of the body, I am more able to appreciate the journey and laugh at it frequently.

With no fear of death or judgment, there's no hurry to fix anything and no need to frantically try to control the outcome of any situation. My hope is that the teachings in this book will help you make small shifts in your awareness so that you can experience this sense of timelessness, which will allow the voice of your soul and your own guides to come through.

1. There is No Death

"You're on the deck of a boat watching dolphins play. The dolphins arc up above the surface, and then dive under the water, disappearing from your sight. Isn't there something inside you that *knows* the dolphins still exist? Somehow you know that they're just completing that circle under the surface, even though you can't see them anymore. You don't worry that they're gone forever. You know they're *somewhere;* they've simply moved between worlds and they're coming back, whether you're there to witness their return or not. Above, below, above again. Why wouldn't it also be so with death?"

- Mary McDonald-Lewis

The way we perceive death is a *choice.*

When my 10 year-old son Danny was diagnosed with a degenerative illness that would end his life sometime within the next 10 years, we began a sacred, transcendent journey that led us through disability, death and beyond. A large piece of this process involved my helping him to understand life and death in a way that would give meaning to his life and help him face his death without fear.

As his illness progressed, he lost the ability to speak, and by age 12 was unable to talk in full sentences. We were never able to have an "adult" discussion about death, so I had to feel my way intuitively through his perceptions, emotions and life experience in the hope of discovering whatever beliefs and images he held about the end of physical life.

Like most American children, the only information Danny had about death came from television, movies and video games. Although he couldn't verbalize this, I imagined that he thought of death as a violent, angry, terrifying event. He'd never known anybody who'd died, not even a pet. His grandparents were alive and well, and

7

although some of the elders in our family had died, they were virtual strangers to him.

Once, when Danny was about six years old, he told me that when people die they go to "Ghost City," a magical place "where kids can drive cars and go to school to learn about fun stuff." When Danny began facing his own death, I wondered if this precious image was still in his mind. Thankfully, our family legacy was not a religious one, so we were free from visions of everlasting torture in hell or a Heaven filled exclusively with saved Christians. Danny's mind was completely open, which gave me a rare opportunity to fill it with beautiful, peaceful images, free of fear and judgment.

During the last years of Danny's life I searched libraries and websites for material on positive, non-judgmental traditions and mythologies about death, and was particularly drawn to Buddhist and Native American stories. I read these stories to Danny, and imparted to him a vision of death and the afterlife that resonated with my own heart, incorporating my personal belief in reincarnation, the essence of our spirits and the possibility of communication between dimensions.

As I wrote in my previous book, *A Swan in Heaven,* "At night I lay by his side singing to him and telling him that I would be OK on earth without him and would see him very soon. I told him that in the spirit realms he could have any kind of body he wanted, and he could visit me anytime, and neither of us would be lonely because our souls would still be together. I explained how there was no such thing as linear time on the other side, and that people can be in more than one place at the same time. I told him everything I knew, everything I'd learned in my metaphysical studies, hoping he'd understand and wouldn't be afraid of dying."

Religious doctrine, literature, sacred hymns and ageless folk songs impart nightmarish imagery of a "cold, lonesome grave," the "icy hand of death" and "the dreary regions of the dead." Add images of turning to dust, being eaten by worms and a 50/50 chance of an eternity in hell, and the fear of death is securely seated in the minds of many children by the age of six.

Even the blissful images of death keep us from a meaningful understanding of the sacred transition from physical to non-physical existence. Sitting next to Jesus on a throne or floating on a cloud playing a harp for eternity doesn't explain or justify our purpose on earth, and offers us a stagnant, rather pointless afterlife. This leaves us with three basic ideas about death (which will be explored in more detail later in this chapter):

1. Judgment - We'll go to a good place or a bad place depending on our behavior.

2. Separation - We'll be away from loved ones, where we can't be contacted.

3. Permanence- We're gone forever, and all life experience stops.

An innate fear of death is at the root of all neurosis. The ego's terror of extinction is the driving force behind extreme behaviors that are designed to establish dominance and control, such as violence, war, abuse, corruption and bigotry. This is not only true for individuals; it's true for families, governments, religions, corporations and nations. The ego cries out, "What will become of ME?" and acts from an instinctive fear of disappearance and loss of identity. One could think of this as a survival instinct, but it begs the question... what, exactly, is trying to survive?

I talked with a woman recently whose teenage daughter was dying from a rare disease. She said to me unapologetically, "I *like* my separateness. I don't want to merge into the void. I don't want to relinquish my individual identity."

That's the voice of the human ego talking. It's the *personality* wanting to survive, to be recognized and to be in control. The soul knows that it can't disappear, but the ego -- the personality -- lives in fear of annihilation. On the soul level we are eternal; we are parts of the whole, like a blob of mercury from which pieces can pull away but are always magnetically drawn back to their source. Our souls have individual paths, histories and intentions that are acted out when we break off from the source into separate bodies during our incarnations. Our bodies are the "experiential" aspects of that source, but we are never actually separate, and always return to Source via dreams, visions, meditation or death. Because we live in a multi-dimensional reality, we don't disappear after death, but continue to resonate on a higher frequency. Embracing this view can help us release fear-based notions of punishment rather than correction, judgment rather than support, and an eternity of idleness rather than limitless opportunity for growth.

This view also gives us a new way of understanding and processing grief. I know a man whose son died in a train collision at age 16. The boy was a talented actor and compassionate animal activist. The father laments that his son died before he could fulfill his potential in these areas, and sees his son's death as the tragic "waste" of a life that could have contributed so much to the world. But our existence can never be wasted if the work of our souls continues after death. It's as if we worked for a company and got transferred to a branch office in a new city, doing the same work in a different location. This young man's love of art and animals, along with the gifts, lessons and growth tools he provided to his loved ones, continues now in another form, and his life is far from over. The guidance, love and energy he radiates from the Other Side provides boundless gifts of awareness and expansion for his loved ones on earth as well as members of his soul family in the non-physical.

We've all heard the cliché, "nobody's ever come back from death to tell us about it, so there's no proof that the soul lives on." But that's not true. Countless people have had near-death experiences and communication with departed loved ones, and there are hundreds of books on the subject. The Gallup poll reports that between 72% and 83% of Americans believe in Heaven,[1] 21% communicate mentally with someone who has died,[2] 78% believe in angels[3] and 20% believe in reincarnation.[4] Some reports indicate that between 5 and 30 percent

---

[1] http://www.gallup.com/poll/11770/Eternal-Destinations-Americans-Believe-Heaven-Hell.aspx
[2] http://www.gallup.com/poll/16915/Three-Four-Americans-Believe-Paranormal.aspx
[3] http://www.gallup.com/poll/11770/Eternal-Destinations-Americans-Believe-Heaven-Hell.aspx
[4] http://www.gallup.com/poll/16915/Three-Four-Americans-Believe-Paranormal.aspx

of people have had near-death experiences.[5] When you consider how many people that is (and the numbers are likely to be much higher than surveys actually record), there's actually more proof in favor of a world beyond the body than against it.

I began receiving "interdimensional" messages from my son less than an hour after his death. These dialogs continue to this day, and they guide the work I'm now doing as an author and spiritual teacher. I'm certain that the conversations Danny and I had about death during the last years of his life are what made this possible. We looked at death a certain way and it became our reality. *The way we perceive death is a choice.* If we believe in hell and judgment, we will carry that belief to our deaths and to the deaths of our loved ones, and the death experience will be filled with stress and fear. If we believe that death is the continuation of a rich, expansive journey, then the experience can be understood and enlightening for everyone involved.

HOW WE LEARN ABOUT DEATH

Most urban Americans never see a dead body unless it's embalmed and dressed up for a funeral. But in many other cultures and in rural communities, people are exposed to death throughout their lives. In countries suffering from war or famine, in tribal societies, in cultures that accept death and in places where people live close to the land, death is neither hidden nor sanitized.

During my childhood, when an aged relative died, the younger children weren't allowed to go to the funerals because the adults thought it would be too upsetting. When I became a mother I could see the flaw in this logic, and true to my role as the black sheep of the family, I encouraged my adult siblings and cousins to take their little ones to these funerals, recognizing these events as opportunities to teach children about the cycles of life and death. My family's preference for avoidance and suppression did more to create fear and superstition in the children than to protect them from it.

---

[5] http://www.metaphysical-news-and-views.com/near-death-experiences.html

It's probably fair to say that most people view death in one of these three ways:

1. Heaven and Hell

We have one life to live on earth but our souls live on after death, and if we follow the rules of our culture and our religion, we will be rewarded after death with a conflict-free eternity, recognized by our god and our peers as a good or righteous person. If we don't follow these rules, we will be judged for our sins and sentenced to an eternity in a place of terror from which there is no return or redemption. *When dying or grieving, this view leaves us terrified that we may have failed in life, and gives no reason for our experiences on earth other than an ultimate reward or punishment after death.*

2. There is nothing beyond physical existence

This view holds that there is no such thing as a non-physical world. When we die, our bodies decompose and we're gone forever. There is no soul or spirit, and no afterlife. The physical body is all there is, and after it dies, there is nothing left. A lifetime of achievements, relationships, growth experiences and creations remains frozen in time, because this one lifetime was our only encounter with existence. *When dying or grieving, this view leaves us feeling utterly abandoned as victims of random chaos in a finite system. It also exacerbates the feeling of permanent loss for the bereaved, making the grief process more difficult.*

3. The soul lives on for the exclusive purpose of growth and awakening

The soul continues to broadcast its energy after the body dies. It moves along its journey, sometimes embodied during incarnations and at other times disembodied, continuing its work from non-physical realms. The soul lives on as part of the human panorama, but in an unseen dimension. *When dying or grieving, this view gives purpose to one's life on earth, and provides limitless opportunities for expansion, correction and creation, no matter how short or how tragic the current physical life might have been.*

Whatever your belief system may be, the ideas you absorbed as a child were handed down by your family, your culture, your social circle and your religion (your tribe). This includes information gleaned from television, movies, books, art, educational institutions and other sources. But as you evolved as an individual and were exposed to new information, you used your free will and critical thinking skills to blend new ideas with your childhood beliefs, thus creating your own personal theology. When I was a child, my tribe told me that God punishes bad people and rewards good people. Observation, education and experience eventually showed me that this wasn't true, and I gradually moved out of that belief. It's an evolutionary process in which we choose to keep some ideas and reject others according to where we are along our spiritual paths. But in the beginning of each earthly incarnation, these beliefs are *given* to us according to tribal tradition.

The fear of death-- which translates into the fear of judgment and punishment for many people -- is one of those beliefs. And it's more commonly held than you might imagine. When Pope John Paul II died in 2005, news reports showed millions of people crying the world over. He was 84 years old and very ill. His death was peaceful and expected. His life was meaningful. *So why were they crying?* Surely they felt confident that he'd go to Heaven, so they probably weren't worried about his soul. Did the death of someone considered to be pious and holy force millions of Catholics to feel inadequate by comparison and come face-to-face with their fears about Hell?

THE LANGUAGE PROBLEM

I conduct a wonderful little exercise in my workshops that's a spin-off on the "telephone game" that many of us played as children. In this schoolyard game, a group of kids form a line, and the person at the front of the line whispers a story to the person next to her, and that person whispers it to the next, and that person to the next, and so on down the line. At the end of the game, the last person to hear the story recites it to the group, and it is barely recognizable as the original story told by the first person in line.

The variation of this exercise in my workshops illustrates the value of *discernment* and *intuition* in helping determine what we believe to be true. In this exercise, I ask three people to leave the room, and while they're gone I tell the rest of the group a story, usually a Native American death or creation myth.

Then the first person from outside is brought in and a member of the group recounts the story. After that, the second person is brought in, and the first person tells the story to the second person. After that, the second person tells the story to the third person

As you might expect, by the time the story reaches the third person, the names of the characters have been either changed or omitted, details have been modified, timelines skewed, words replaced, and the entire meaning of the story lost. All it took was four people and 20 minutes. Imagine what happens to stories that travel through thousands of people and hundreds of years.

When I conduct this exercise, I intentionally choose the oldest person in the room, the youngest person and a non-native English speaker, because this is how we received most of our religious teachings; translated from language to language and handed down orally from elders to children. These teachings were also carried across ever-changing political and linguistic borders, and were frequently altered according to the personal preferences of the storyteller. By the time writing and printing became possible, the original stories were altered beyond recognition. The teachings of the Buddha were shared orally for 400 years before they were ever written down. The book of Exodus in the Old Testament was written centuries after the events supposedly took place, and the earliest recorded gospel of the New Testament was written at least 40 years after the death of Jesus. There were numerous other documents written at the time, but these were rejected in the first and second centuries by the founders of the church in order to create a cohesive, controllable belief system. By the fourth century the surviving material was revised even further by the Emperor Constantine because it didn't fit neatly into his vision of a Christian Rome.

Many words have a specific meaning in one language during one period in history, but end up with a completely different meaning at another time, in another place, in another language. The English word "Heaven" for example, is derived from a Middle English word that means to "heave or throw." This word is related to the Old English word "hebben," which refers to a handle one uses to raise an object, which may relate to the cliché of moving Heaven and earth. The Middle English word "hevi" refers to a state of "heaviness," which has to do with heaving, as in "lifting up," and this translated into the word "Heaven," referring to something that resides up in the sky above us.[6] But what was the *original* word from the various Bible translations that spanned Aramaic, Coptic, Greek, Hebrew and a thousand other languages over the years? How can we possibly know which word was intended by the original authors, much less its meaning?

To further illustrate this point, here are two versions of widely-recognized *Lord's Prayer*. The first is the familiar King James version (translated from Greek). The second is a translation from Aramaic (the language Jesus spoke) to English:

Our Father which art in Heaven,
Hallowed be thy name.
Thy kingdom come.
Thy will be done in earth, as it is in Heaven.
Give us this day our daily bread.
And forgive us our debts, as we forgive our debtors.
And lead us not into temptation, but deliver us from evil.
For thine is the kingdom, and the power, and the glory, forever.

And here is a translation (one of several) to English from Aramaic:[7]

---

[6] ORIGINS, A Short Etymological Dictionary of Modern English - by Eric Partridge
[7] http://www.astramate.com/lordsprayer.htm

O Birther! Father-Mother of the Cosmos,
you create all that moves in light.
O Thou! The breathing Life of all,
Creator of the Shimmering Sound that touches us.

Respiration of all worlds,
we hear you breathing-in and out in silence.

Source of Sound: in the roar and the whisper,
in the breeze and the whirlwind, we hear your Name.

Radiant One: You shine within us,
outside us-even darkness shines-when we remember.

Name of names, our small identity
unravels in you, you give it back as a lesson.

Wordless Action, Silent Potency-
where ears and eyes awaken, there Heaven comes.

O Birther! Father-Mother of the Cosmos!

The Aramaic version sounds almost Buddhist or Native American, and the references to sound, light and breath feel *inclusive,* as if God is right inside us, or very near rather than off in some inaccessible, obscure location in the sky.

When these translations are researched even further, it turns out that there are several different translations in each language, depending on the perspective of the translator. One version of The Lord's prayer translated from Aramaic to English mentions bread, vines and a trinity.[8] So which version of this -- and everything we've been taught about life, death, Heaven and hell -- should we accept?

---

[8] http://www.astramate.com/lordsprayer.htm

The point of this little exercise is to show that semantics is always a problem when it comes to ancient teachings, which is exactly why we have nothing to rely on but our *intuition*... the resonance of our souls with the meanings of scriptures, myths and legends. Our intuitive skills are the only tools we have for sorting through the ideas that are presented to us throughout our lives, and the only way to know what is true is to listen to our souls speaking to us *directly*. And when we replace traditional notions with our own innate sense of truth, it is possible for intuition to remove *fear,* especially as it relates to death.

One of the myths we work with in the telephone game is an Inuit creation story in which a young warrior steals the sun, moon and stars from the lodge of a greedy chief who wants to keep these things for himself. The warrior carries the celestial bodies into the sky and places them there, and that's how the sun, moon and stars were created.

This story is no more believable than the idea that when we die our deeds are examined and we are sent to one of two places in remote, non-physical locations for the rest of eternity. In this system, there is no opportunity for growth, correction or healing because we were given one chance and a limited period of time in which to prove ourselves (to whom?). If we blow it, we are done forever.

But what if there's no time limit? What if there's no *time?*

The other day while waiting in my dentist's office I flipped through a beautifully illustrated book about the human body. The book was published by a worldwide mega-publisher, and I was delighted -- for a moment -- to find that it contained a section on near-death experiences (NDEs). It quoted various scientific theories about how NDEs might be the result of either the brain's neurotransmitters shutting down, a lack of oxygen to the brain, or REM and dream activity. One theory suggests that the tunnel experienced by many NDEers is simply a memory of coming through the birth canal. The writer summarized by saying that NDEs are probably just a spectacular final fireworks show produced by the brain in the last seconds before we go into oblivion.

If there is not a consciousness that lives beyond physical life and we have only one lifetime on earth (even if we only live for a few seconds after birth), then what's the point in even examining these questions? If we come from oblivion and return to oblivion with a short span of time in between, then we aren't actually coming or going *anywhere* on this journey. The whole journey would be pointless.

In David Staume's marvelous book, *The Atheist Afterlife,* he explains the energetic changes that occur when we go from physical to non-physical existence. He asks us to imagine that we are in a car that has just lost control and is sailing off the edge of a cliff. Using a basic rule of physics that "any energy unable to express itself in its current form will transition into another form," the energy of the car hurling toward the ground will, upon impact, be transformed into fire, heat, debris, dust and sound... other forms of energy. Meanwhile, assuming you die in this crash, your non-physical self (your soul, essence, consciousness, mind, spirit, life force, astral body or whatever you choose to call it) will follow the same law of physics and will not disappear, but will *transform.*

Staume says: "If the relationship between your body and your consciousness is the same as that between the car and the energy of movement, your consciousness wouldn't be extinguished either; it would behave like every other energy in the universe; it would obey the law of Conservation of Energy[9] and it would *transition*."

An analogy even an atheist could love, assuming said atheist believes that there *is* a consciousness separate from the body. But when we start to question where the consciousness actually *goes*, the going gets tough, because this is where theology comes in and drives everybody to their respective corners.

The problem with talking about an afterlife is that most people see it as exclusively enmeshed with religion, and this causes instant contention. There are two reasons why the idea of life after death is always tied to religion: because all religious doctrines talk about an afterlife, and because the only information we ever get about an afterlife is within the context of religion. It's hopelessly tied up in

---

[9] From Wikipedia: The law of conservation of energy states that the total amount of energy in an isolated system remains constant. A consequence of this law is that energy cannot be created or destroyed. The only thing that can happen with energy in an isolated system is that it can change form, that is to say for instance kinetic energy can become thermal energy.

circular reasoning; a perpetual myth-making machine. The idea of a *non-religious* afterlife would do wonders for helping humanity lose its fear of death, but as long as the idea is only understood in a fear-based religious context, it will continue to frighten us. If the soul is eternal and we live over and over again in different bodies, locations, cultures and environments specifically chosen to help our souls grow, then life actually *means something.* If we are allowed endless "do-overs" and endless time for correction (rather than a one-and-only final punishment or reward), and if we're not graded on performance, then perhaps our primal fear of death wouldn't be so pervasive and we could stop living our lives like nervous kids getting ready to take their college entrance exams. If the clock isn't ticking and we're not being watched and judged, maybe we wouldn't be so panicked about competing with each other, being right, clinging to people, possessions and ideas, forcing our will onto others and fighting desperately for a secure foothold on earth and in Heaven.

Most of us have experienced dreams, visions and impressions that feel as if we've been contacted by loved ones on the Other Side. Many of us have experienced flashes of thought, sounds, verbal phrases, kinetic events, music or scents that we felt were sent by some sort of "higher" force, be it departed loved ones, angels or guides. And although the majority of people believe in an afterlife and in angels, most don't believe that contact is possible, and they dismiss these experiences as coincidences, oddities or freak events.

But if we trust these experiences, if we trust what *feels true,* we can be led to a whole new way of seeing our world, including the world beyond the physical. What's the point of spiritual work -- seeking, praying, meditating and studying -- if not to help ourselves find peace? We are just as able to choose a theology of fear as a theology of love, and in doing so, we can begin to see that in death there is no disappearance and no loss of identity. And in seeing that, a great peace, grace and acceptance can come into our lives, changing the way we live *and* die.

2. God: A New Story

Q: How can God let this terrible thing happen?
A: It depends on what you think God *is*.

At some point in your childhood, if you grew up in Judeo-Christian America, you began learning about God, creation, the Ten Commandments, Heaven and Hell, Jesus, Moses, the Bible, Hanukah, Santa Claus or some combination of the above. And if the Old Testament was part of your childhood teachings (especially if you actually *read* any of it), you may have gotten the impression that God is constantly angry and disappointed in us because we are unworthy, sinful, marred and imperfect and can't live up to his demands and expectations. A God who wipes out humanity with a flood, murders those who don't follow his rules and encourages genocide against the inhabitants of land he claims for his "chosen" people presents a scary picture. Many of us -- especially those who were raised with strict religious backgrounds -- grew up feeling that we did something wrong just by being born and that we have to work hard all our lives to get back into God's good graces. And maybe if we hit all the right buttons and do all the right things, God won't be mad at us anymore and we'll get to go to Heaven.

While this mindset may not be obvious in our outward behavior, it plants invisible, insidious seeds of self-loathing and inadequacy in our thinking, and belittles the dignity of our souls and our very existence. If we're always worried about the King of the Universe being angry with us, we don't have much chance to recognize Divine Love when it's right in front of us. If we're lucky enough to see through this at some point, some of us may become spiritual seekers, but others will be turned off to spirituality of any kind, which eliminates the Divine from our lives completely and leaves us spiritually bereft. It's a lot of pain to live with, and it's all because of a childhood wound caused by the lie that we are not one with God and that we are so separate it is actually possible for God to *judge us.*

This is the story most of us were told as children, and it implies that we have a limited amount of time in which to please God before we die, and only one chance to do this for all of eternity. We will either succeed or fail, but either way, we only have only one shot at it. So we plod through our lives doing the best we can, and even though we're good people and follow all the rules, bad things still happen to us. Our hearts get broken, we lose our jobs, our spouses abandon or abuse us, our children get killed by drunk drivers, we get sick or depressed and have the same experiences that everybody else has, despite our belief that if we're "good" we'll be protected from trauma. But trauma happens anyway, and we think, "Hey, this isn't supposed to happen. I did all the right things. I'm a good person and God's supposed to be nice to me. There must be something wrong with me. I failed in some way, because no matter what I do, I still feel powerless and unsafe, and nothing can fix it; not getting baptized or doing community service or donating to charity or saving the whales... *nothing.*"

Of course nothing can fix it. Because it isn't broken.

These so-called "bad" experiences are part of the soul's journey and the program we signed on for when we chose incarnation. The experience of pain and conflict is as much a gift as the experience of joy and security. We are here to accumulate experience for the purpose of growth and expansion, and the pain, isolation and powerlessness we feel at times can be understood in different ways depending on how we look at it. The biggest error in our thinking is in perceiving God as an authority figure, like a stern parent who disciplines us by dispensing reward and punishment for our behavior. How different would our life experiences be if we saw God not as a parent, but as a *partner?* An energy-generating source that supports our growth in whatever way we create it, via whatever experiences we create, offering nothing but unconditional love? Rather than a watchful figure standing over us in judgment, what if God is simply an energy of love and light that *doesn't have an opinion?*

This is a new story about God. Not the Old Testament God who was a heartless tyrant that flew into murderous rages at the drop of a hat. Not the God who pulls all the strings and holds all the cards while we tremble in fear. Not the God who likes some of us better than others, tells us what to do and punishes us if we don't obey. That God doesn't allow mistakes, which means there is only a limited time to learn, grow and heal. We get one lifetime, and that lifetime ends in final judgment. If we don't get it right by the time we die, we don't get a second chance. Three strikes and we're out. Game over. Forever.

The personality of God shifted when Jesus came along for many reasons. Humans were evolving, and it was time for the angry god to step aside and allow a more heart-based spirituality to emerge. The Old Testament didn't speak much about an afterlife, but with Jesus we began to think about life beyond the physical plane. He knew all about the many levels and frequencies on which we exist, and he also knew that God is not a free-standing entity that lives in a separate world, but is an energetic force of light and love, of which we are all part. I like to think that Jesus came here as an *intervention,* because he could see that we had it all wrong. And he wasn't the only great master to do this, though he certainly became the most popular. There were countless others in human history (and many living among us today) who teach us to see God in a different way… as an unconditionally forgiving, infinitely patient *energy* that fuels our growth and could never, ever judge us. It cannot judge us because it is not separate from us. In order to judge we have to stand back and observe something that is separate from ourselves. We have to be able to see it from a distance. And God is not distant enough for that to happen.

Jesus was all about changing the way people perceive God, and he said, "It's not about form, it's not about how many days you fast, or cowering before God or sacrificing to God. It's about knowing God as God lives inside you, which means knowing that you already *are* in a state of love. I call God my father and call myself his son to show that you that we are *all* sons and daughters of this love force called 'God,' and we all possess the same light, the same love and the same power."

But people still felt bullied by the old angry God who smote them with everything from earthquakes to hemorrhoids for the slightest infractions, so the gentle God introduced by Jesus was difficult to accept. It was unfathomable that a Hebrew, a Roman, an Ethiopian or a leper could be as worthy of Divine gifts as a prophet or a priest.

Yet that's exactly what Jesus was telling us. He was talking about *oneness.* God is an energy that fuels the life force, and it is, essentially, neutral. We are sparks of that life force, like the pieces of mercury that keep returning to their source, temporarily split off into human bodies on earth until we return home again via physical death. The concepts of Heaven and Hell simply refer to the states of mind we experience when we are either aligned with the flow of love (Heaven/God), or resisting and doubting it in fear (Hell/Satan).

There *is* nothing else.

We wonder how to justify the incomprehensible death of a child caught in the crossfire of a drive-by shooting, the annihilation of entire communities from natural disasters, or the decimation of a culture by greed and political corruption. From the perspective of our physical bodies at ground level, which is subject to the whims of the ego, these events seem unexplainable. But in the view from the higher realms, from the soul level, we understand it perfectly. The human personality sees unbearable pain and discomfort, but the soul knows that spending time in "earth school" experiencing selected hardships is a matter of the right tool for the right job. From the soul's perspective, the more effective a package we create for growth, the more potent the growth is. Heaven doesn't have any judgment about a good life vs. a bad life, or a just death vs. an unjust death. There are no rewards or punishments. <u>There is no judgment anywhere in the universe.</u> Whatever serves the evolution of soul -- which translates into the evolution of *whole* -- is the greatest gift and the highest blessing.

We suffer on earth because we think we're alone. That's why relationships are the hardest thing we deal with in human life, because in relationships we are at our most vulnerable and most willing to be led by our hearts. If only we could see that the relationships we choose are representative of our soul's desire to merge with Home, with the oneness, with the blob of mercury, the place where we are always safe.

The ones we love are part of us, and since we're all one energy, we're really merging with ourselves, with the great One Self, merging with God/Source/Home.

Perhaps the histrionics of the Old Testament God was a statement about our separation from Home. Maybe those stories were written to illustrate the birth of the human ego, which believes that it operates alone, without the support of the higher realms, so God was angry that we tried to live without full awareness of our connection to Home. But if the authors of the Old Testament intended to say that, then wouldn't they have created a God that gently guided us back toward the light?

And if our ultimate goal is to merge back to the source, why would we have chosen to separate in the first place?

"The choice to separate can be compared to the desire to travel the world or to go on an archeological expedition. The choice made by the particular group of entities that became the human race was nothing more dramatic than that. The expansion of consciousness is a natural force in the universe and it cannot be stopped, so our choice to go on an expedition was part of that expansion. It was a desire to acquire new experience in order to feed the constant expansion of the universe. Physicists will tell you that universe has two basic movements... expansion and contraction. This is the expansion part.

The contraction took place when we, as a collective, focused intently on creating forms in which to take this journey. We created physical bodies by directing our energy with enough determination, unity and resolve that we were able to manifest physical matter in the form of bodies. The earth and the planets were created this way as well, and this is what is meant in Genesis when it speaks of "God" creating these things. Yes, God created them, if you understand God to be the collective energy and focused force of all the thought forms at all the levels of consciousness in the universe. Thought *is* that powerful. So this collective desire moved us into the earth plane, and gave us physical bodies in order to have the experiences we sought.

This is what happens in every individual incarnation. While it might appear that we are separated from Source when we are in bodies, we are not truly separate. We simply have to *densify* -- to make our energy heavier and more physical -- in order to survive on the earth plane. In doing so, we forfeit some of our ability to resonate on the higher planes, and this produces a sensation that feels like a separation from God/Home/Source. The mystics, shamans and seers throughout history have attempted to describe this sensation of separation though the use of symbols, parables and mythologies, such as the story of Adam and Eve being banished from the Garden of Eden, or God being disappointed in his creations and sending a flood to wipe the whole thing out and start over again. These are *separation allegories*.

But we are never truly separated, because there are fibers that connect us. The door is always open and the conduit is always there. We came to earth originally in a state similar to that of a newborn baby, retaining a vague memory of Home/Heaven, as all children do. As we matured as a species we became aware of a subtle and inexplicable sense of loss, and in an effort to explain and understand it, we created our mythologies, which include creation stories, separation allegories and symbolic representations of death."

GRIEF, LOSS, GOOD AND EVIL

In my work as a grief guidance facilitator, I've walked the grief journey with individuals from every religious perspective. Those who've lost a loved one in a tragic manner have one primary question... *"Why would a loving God let this happen?"*

The answer depends what you think God *is*.

If we see God as a connective fiber that links every action in the universe in an interdependent movement toward wholeness, then there's no reason why this force would shield us from discomfort and conflict. To expect God to behave like a protective mother hen is an infantile view that further separates and disempowers us. If we think that God's love is supposed to provide us with a conflict-free existence, we will always be disappointed. Because when that expectation is not met -- and it can *never* be met -- we end up focusing more on our feelings of anger and abandonment than on the valuable lessons these experiences were designed to teach us.

Instead of wondering why bad things are allowed to happen, consider instead that there are no "good" or "bad" things in the universe, only the creations that move us forward in our evolution. We cannot judge these creations, because they are necessary in order for growth and expansion to occur. They are there to provide traction, something to push against, like a swimmer pushing off the edge of a pool.

Whenever this topic comes up in one of my workshops, someone inevitably raises the question of good and evil, and along with it, a mention of the poster boy for all evil -- Adolph Hitler. The idea of good and evil is difficult to give up because it's so tied to judgment, and people are very attached to judgment. In these same dialogs I'm often asked why people have to die in war, plane crashes, floods, famines and terrorist attacks. And I've been known to answer, "Why is it better to live here on earth than at home in Heaven?"

If you understand that we are more than just these physical bodies and we exist in multiple dimensions, it's easy to see how the revolving door between this world and the next simply carries us from one classroom to another in the continuing education of our souls. Death is like waking up from a dream and finding yourself comfortably at home in your own bed. If we relinquish the idea that God judges us and replace it with a self-empowered view in which everything is connected and happens for a specific reason, then the Hitlers and the Mother Teresas of the world are all part of a magnificent Divine dance of *balance*. Stillness vs. disruption, order vs. chaos, yin vs. yang, expansion vs. contraction… all of it leads ultimately to Oneness.

This dispassionate attitude about death was illustrated for me once in the most unlikely of places. It was a rerun of the old television show *Kung Fu* with David Carradine. His character, Kwai Chang Caine, was a Buddhist priest traveling in 1870s America who had to contend with drunken cowboys, vicious thieves and angry mobs wherever he went. Foolhardy men were always picking fights with him (which naturally he'd win, because he was Kung Fu Master). In an episode I watched just a few years ago, the sheriff warned him to get out of town before the angry mob caught up with him. The sheriff shouted, "If you don't leave now, you'll die!" Caine just shrugged with calm detachment while playing his flute and said, "So. I will die."

"There is a different way to understand the concept of harmony vs. conflict. In the natural world on earth, the ecosystem works in perfect harmony, but it requires conflict. A wolf must eat a rabbit, and while the wolf is chasing the rabbit, the rabbit is in a state of panic; it is not peaceful, and the whole situation is quite violent. Yet this is perfect harmony in nature.

The same is true in human experience. Is it a natural part of the human ecosystem when thousands of humans are killed in an earthquake? It's just like the wolf killing the rabbit. Without these so-called "negative" experiences, we would have no swimming pool edge from which to push off. The souls involved in these experiences have chosen this as part of their contribution to the evolution of the human species. They are members of a soul group that has agreed to this experience for a number of reasons, one of which is to serve as volunteers who help awaken and enlighten the rest of humanity." [10]

The universe holds itself together by exerting opposing forces upon itself, and there is cause and effect in everything. It expands and contracts constantly, because there has to be something to push off *from.* In Glenda Green's magnificently channeled book, *Love Without End: Jesus Speaks,* she receives this amazing explanation of the necessity for conflict:

"In order for faith to be forged, there has to be a profound threat to one's certainty through great compression of conflicting situations... faith and consciousness are both forged under similar circumstances. Once a soul has achieved both faith and consciousness, there is no further need to remain in the confusion of conflicting reality. Until then, it is necessary for you to live at the level of man's varied experiences, feelings and challenges where both your faith and your consciousness may be awakened and fulfilled."

---

[10] The concept of "volunteers" is explained in more detail in Chapter 3.

I recently received an email from someone who was concerned about her friend's difficult pregnancy. She asked the email recipients to pray that the pregnancy that the baby would be born healthy. While I understand her desire for a happy outcome, I also know that the only prayer worth making is a prayer that says, "lead me to the highest possible truth in this situation." Some of us are led to truth by having healthy children, and some of us are led to truth by having seriously ill children or no children at all. From the soul's point of view, one experience is not better or worse than the other. All that matters is the growth plan of the soul.

Contrary to what millions of people came to believe after reading the book *The Secret,* everything we create in our lives is a successful and perfect manifestation, even if it doesn't make us happy. If we're manifesting poverty, illness, struggle and loss, it's because our souls are seeking the growth lessons brought through those experiences. If it serves our soul's evolution to be homeless, then these are lessons we put it into our life plans, and they can't be short-circuited. The law of attraction is not just about attracting the fun, easy stuff. We can only attract what our souls are crying out for -- the stuff we came to earth for -- and these things usually don't match up with what our egos prefer. The true secret is to recognize these experiences as growth opportunities rather than tragedies, and work with them from that angle. Every tragedy gives us a chance to practice releasing fear and opening up to Divine guidance, and that practice leads us back to oneness with the energy known as God.

THE EGO VS. THE SOUL

I've been talking lot about ego vs. soul, it and warrants some explanation.

There are two primary aspects of us at work when we're incarnated. Let's call them the *earth* aspect and the *Heaven* aspect. The earth aspect (which we'll call the *ego* or the *personality*) deals exclusively with managing life on the physical plane. It is responsible for the body's survival, and in order to do that, it must possess certain skills and characteristics. The ego needs to be competitive for example, in order to get the best job, the best mate or the best grades at college. It needs to accumulate wealth and security in order to feel safe. It needs to be aggressive in order to acquire food, sex, dominance over others and anything needed to establish a sense of control over its environment. The ego needs to make judgments in order to create the necessary boundaries and divisions that make it feel secure and in control.

The Heaven aspect (which we'll call the *soul* or *higher self*) is concerned with earth experience only insofar as it serves the soul's blueprint for growth. The soul is who we are in Heaven, when we're Home, connected to Source/God .[11]

The soul doesn't care if the body is beautiful or disfigured, rich or poor, healthy or diseased. It surveys the scene from an elevated perspective and chooses scenarios and situations that will bring forth the greatest experience of universal love. The soul knows exactly what will serve its growth and the growth of the whole. That is the soul's only intention.

The ego, which only wants to survive on earth, kicks and screams against what the soul creates. Because it can't see beyond the dense realm of earth, the ego thinks it's alone in the universe. It doesn't want to lose control, so it experiences fear, greed, manipulation, clinging and panic, while the soul experiences only *trust*. The ego doesn't want to die, but the soul knows there is no death.

Throughout life on earth these forces are in opposition to one another, like in the cartoon images of the devil sitting on one shoulder and an angel sitting on another whispering conflicting prompts into each of your ears. The friction between the soul and the ego is where the idea of God vs. The Devil came from. It's expressed symbolically throughout western theology in a thousand ways, from Adam and Eve's expulsion from the garden to Satan's fall from Heaven and every story in which somebody disobeyed a direct command from God. These stories represent the struggle between the soul and the ego. In

---

[11] More about the how the soul and the body work together during incarnation can be found in Chapter 3.

the *Kung Fu* episodes, Caine is the voice of the soul, and the angry mob is the voice of the ego!

In order to survive on earth, the ego must be present, but the soul is always in the picture, prompting and prodding us from behind the scenes like a proud parent cheering on a child in a school play. The goal of spiritual practice is to align the ego and the soul. The ability to receive Divine communication is absolutely dependent on knowing and accepting this truth.

The soul knows that it's eternal and always connected to Source, but the ego is so busy trying to survive that it has little or no sense of that connection, so it feels panicked and fights even harder for a sense of control over its world.

To understand this, imagine a warrior or soldier who believes he has to force others to comply with the beliefs and customs of his culture, whether it's tribal traditions, religious doctrines or political ideologies. He believes he is doing this to support and honor his culture, and he feels justified killing, torturing and enslaving people for this purpose. This is an expression of his ego's fear of death; the fear of separateness and aloneness in the universe. He does not know that he's one with God and with other humans (if he did, he couldn't justify killing and enslaving them), and this causes great psychic pain. So in order to feel less alone, he needs to bring others into that pain with him, into his belief in separateness.

Religious wars are fought on the premise that "my culture knows what's best for you, and if you don't agree, you must be eliminated, because your presence is a challenge to my sense of security in the universe." So the warrior projects his fear of extinction onto others by eliminating *them.* He is then temporarily relieved of his discomfort. He doesn't realize that this very attitude creates more fear and makes him even more alone, because he now lives in a state where he must constantly defend himself and his culture, and can never be at peace. It's a self-perpetrating cycle that originates with a sense of separation from Source. This is the behavior of the ego.

When humans first separated from Source, it was like leaving a warm house and walking out into an ice storm without protective clothing. The pain and shock of this was unfamiliar, yet it was part of the agreement to take birth and experience other facets of existence. This pain, this "freezing out" by Source, is in our cellular memory and is expressed as the ego's fear of disappearance, or the fear of death (if you believe death to mean complete and permanent separation from life force). It's like being locked out of your house on a freezing day, naked and vulnerable with no way to get back inside.

Throughout the ages humans have had this terror at their core, and from this terror most of the mythologies and religious stories were created, most notably, the Garden of Eden; a separation story that launched the entire Judeo Christian tradition. But as we develop in spiritual practice, we begin to see that the garden goes with us wherever we go. The garden is Home. It is Source, and our departure from it represents our choice to live in the earth realm. But even having made that choice, we can never be separated from Source under any circumstances other than our own belief in the illusion of separation. Once this is understood, we can find peace. We can relax and breathe again... a deep, primal belly breath that echoes the first breath of creation.

Imagine how a very young child would feel if she were lost in a busy place like a shopping mall or an airport, separated from her parents in an immense, crowded, dangerous world. This is how it feels to live on earth without feeling connected to Source/Home, and this is why a life without spiritual awareness and spiritual practice is so empty. It's also the reason for religious wars, because those who are hungry for power and control are the ones who live in the most fear, loneliness, and belief in separation. This is the true definition of Hell.

But where did this start? Why come to earth at all, and why do we forget about Home once we're here?

If we stayed in the warm embrace of Home we wouldn't be able to pile on the learning experiences we accumulate on earth. It is a *choice.* One can choose to go to college and take on a challenging academic program while working at a full time job, struggling for money and studying intensely. There's a lot of stress in a plan like this, but it's a choice one makes when one wants to learn a particular thing. This is how we choose to come to earth.

If we came in with a clear remembrance of Home, we wouldn't be able to tolerate life on earth, because we'd just want to go back and be safe and warm again. The motivation to expand our cumulative experience is stronger than our desire for safety and warmth, and it is a path for which we volunteer. It all balances out because we get to go Home between incarnations, rest up, get strong and be reminded of who/what we are before we dive back into the fray again. We don't have to dive back in if we don't choose to, but everyone living on earth at any given time has chosen it as a curriculum. For some, the curriculum involves a spiritual quest to learn how to balance the ego and soul, and for others it's the experience of the warrior who serves only the ego. Everybody is on a different academic track, but ultimately it all leads to the awareness that we are not separate.

My dear friend Suzy Ward is the author of several books channeled via her son Matthew, who died in 1980. She sends out a newsletter of "Messages From Matthew," and he does a wonderful job of explaining this idea. Here's an excerpt from his April 9, 2009 message:

"Now then, all participants in pre-birth agreements choose their respective roles, which are based in unconditional love for all others in the shared lifetime. Agreements are designed to benefit all the participating souls through their filling gaps in a physical lifetime or completing unfinished karmic lessons, which leads to balanced experiencing. By necessity, the role of some souls is within what is most commonly called "darkness" because it appears to be the opposite of light; but darkness is the *absence* of light, and since light and love are the same energy simply expressed differently, darkness is the *absence of love*. The only way to heal individuals who have been captivated by dark persuasions is by filling their "absence" with love, the original ingredient of all souls.

Now back to the souls who agree to play "dark," or heavy, roles so other souls in the agreement have the opportunity to achieve balance. As an example, when in one lifetime a person is a warrior who tortures and kills an enemy warrior, in another lifetime the two switch places to allow both an opportunity to achieve balance in that respect. And since at soul level, each willingly chooses to play both roles in different lifetimes in order to assist the other, there is reconciliation of the light and the dark. This not only pertains to every one of the billions of souls embodied on the planet, but the countless souls living throughout our universe. When you consider that every celestial body also is a soul, you can understand why the universe is in a constant balancing motion."[12]

We all are moving toward that balanced place together. All the elements are necessary; the warrior, the monk, the slayer and the slain.

---

[12] This and other messages from Matthew can be found at at www.matthewbooks.com.

3. The Journey of the Soul:
A Handbook from Heaven

"Every soul comes to earth connected to every other, and every action is dependent on every other action. We come to earth to further our own growth plans, and sometimes that plan involves serving as a volunteer to sponsor the growth of others. This is often the case when tragic circumstances occur. These beings are volunteering to move their soul families forward in their spiritual evolution. From the soul's perspective, this is never a loss. From the soul's perspective, there are no tragedies."

Danny

In many ways this may be the most important chapter in this book, because it tackles the ponderous questions that theologians, scientists and seekers have been asking for millennia: *What happens when we die? Where did we come from? Why are we here?*

As devoted spiritual seekers, many of us are passionate in our quest to locate a clear, common core at the heart of the world's major religions. We've sampled bits and pieces of them all, cobbling together a patchwork of scraps that expresses our own unique relationships with the Divine. The quest has taken many of us through Judaism and Christianity to Buddhism, Scientology, Atheism and beyond, and now, with our spiritual suitcases covered in travel stickers from ports of call throughout the universe, we realize that we've been longing for Home all along.

Who knew it could be so simple? Like Dorothy in the Wizard of Oz clicking her ruby slippers together, it turns out that Home was following us around the whole time. Guides, angels, ancestors and loved ones on the Other Side, along with all the energy of love and creation that ever existed, are in us and around us all the time, trying to get our attention. Sometimes they scream loudly, smacking us over the head with the proverbial 2x4, and at other times they speak softly in dreams or through music that opens our hearts and brings us to our knees in a flood of tears. But most of the time they simply hover nearby, patiently waiting for us to notice them and allow them to help us find our way Home.

HOMESICK FOR HEAVEN

This place called Home, or Heaven, is not a physical location in the sky. It refers to a vibrational location; a frequency much higher than anything measurable on earth. It is in fact, our natural frequency, and most of us sense fleeting glimpses of it through various channels available to us during our earthly existence. Sometimes these glimpses occur when we experience a sense of perfection and balance in nature, or when coincidences are just too perfect to be random. It happens when we have a déjà vu or a psychic dream, or when we're touched deeply by love or grief. All these flashes and feelings are hints at our constant connection to this Source, our Home. And in that place, there is only Love.

One of the ways we stay connected to Home is through the presence of guides and invisible helpers who walk with us at all times, eager to help us maintain our link to the Divine. In fact, they're so eager that I often imagine them jumping up and down waving their arms frantically trying to get us to notice them, and this is especially true of our loved ones who have died. It's always baffled me that so many people believe in a soul or essence that travels to a spirit world after death, yet they draw the line at believing we can communicate with that world.

We have, without question, the ability to telepathically connect to the vibrational frequency of the place that my guides refer to as Heaven. It's not a remote location in outer space, but is all around us and inside us, and it has very little to do with death as most of us understand death. It is not separate from us, but is *interior,* and is made from the same vibrational substance that creates all energy in the universe. It includes physical and non-physical living things, all thought forms and all possibilities. These energies are vibrant, alive and broadcasting to us constantly, and it's as easy as clicking our ruby slippers together to hear them once we learn how to trust, surrender and receive.

That is the true meaning of *faith*.

So travel with me for a moment and imagine that this connection is available to you, and that it's broadcasting energy and information all the time, like a television or radio. When you're not watching the television, the channels are still broadcasting, are they not? And if you *are* watching, you're tuned into one channel, but the others continue to broadcast even though you're not receiving them at the moment. Danny has dubbed this system "The Interdimensional Postal Service," or the "IPS." Messages, energy and information are delivered between dimensions via the IPS the same way people send physical packages to each other via the UPS (United Parcel Service). They are care packages from Home.

HOW TO GET THERE

The way to receive this information is through meditation, which lightens and ventilates our dense physical forms so that the boundaries between us and Home begin to fade.

One of my favorite meditations begins with a visualization in which you imagine your body as a pencil outline, and then slowly imagine a giant eraser removing the outline until you dissolve into oneness. When you dissolve like that, you touch Heaven. The mystics, sages and teachers throughout human history from every religious tradition have described this, and if you remove the dogma, politics, judgment, separation and "them and us" mentality from religious teachings, you will be looking at that beautiful, pure core where we are one with Source, a.k.a. *God.*

So if the way to call home is through meditation and prayer, then why does a direct connection seem so difficult for so many who meditate and pray? Probably because they're trying too hard. Heaven is so close that if we think too hard about it, work too hard at it, focus too intensely on it or bring in too much expectation, form and structure, we'll miss what's right in front of us.

First, it's important to understand what meditation is and is *not.*

It is *not* sitting up straight, emptying your mind and becoming blank. If you want to hear God and your own soul talking, it's about allowing the cosmic debris to flush through you rather than trying to shut it out. When you sit down to meditate and attempt to quiet your mind (you can also lie down… fetal position works as well as lotus position), your mind is anything but quiet. It's usually reciting a laundry list of earthly concerns (*"I need to change the oil in my car. I don't have my rent this month. My back hurts. Do I look fat in this?"*).

Instead of trying to silence those thoughts, look at each one and follow it to wherever it leads, and pay close attention to its path (you will soon be able to discern which thoughts to follow and which to release). Each thought will lead you on a journey to a thousand new thoughts, seemingly disconnected, that will eventually give birth to an image, idea or phrase that delivers a potent message. I recommend that my students keep paper and pen handy, or better yet, a digital voice recorder to keep track of these impressions. Because those impressions are being sent via the IPS.

One thing that throws us off when we're trying to make this connection is the imagery we've been taught to expect from mystical experiences. Religious scriptures, paintings, literature and Hollywood movies have convinced us that when communicating with other realms we should see winged angels or eerie apparitions, or perhaps the furniture should fly across the room or the lights flicker on and off. While all these things are possible, they are not necessary. Communication with Heaven doesn't always come with special effects.

The best way I can illustrate this is by sharing a revelation I had while working in my garden recently. An old song from the 1940s got stuck in my mind. It was a song called *Scarlet Ribbons,* which my mother used to sing to me when I was a child. It came out of nowhere (though I now know it was sent via the IPS as a teaching tool). In the song, a father peeks in to his daughter's bedroom to say goodnight, and finds her praying, asking God to send her some scarlet ribbons for her hair. The father goes to bed and frets all night because he's too poor to buy ribbons, but miraculously, the next morning, the child wakes to find the ribbons on her bed, and the father has no idea how they got there.

It's a sweet song, but it perpetrates the misconception that prayers are answered with magic tricks. Yes, prayer is answered... *always.* But the answers don't come in the forms we expect. The little girl might pray for scarlet ribbons and the next week her Aunt Zelda comes to visit bearing scarlet ribbons as a gift (with no prompting from the girl's father). Or maybe the girl goes to play at a friend's house and the friend decides to give the girl her own scarlet ribbons as a token of their friendship (as little girls often do). Some people might look at these events as coincidences. But there *are* no coincidences, only co-*creations* manufactured by our higher selves in tandem with the energy of all creation. You can see how this works in your own life. You pray for a new career and a week later you get fired from the miserable job you've hated for years. Now you're free to pursue your new career. *That's* an answered prayer.

There are guides, teachers, angels and others who are waiting to direct us to the answers to our prayers, and they serve us in hundreds of unimaginable ways. They're talking to us all the time, but most of us aren't listening, because we have the crazy idea that God stopped talking to people 2,000 years ago and never said another word. This idea perpetrates terrible desolation and loneliness, because it implies that we're alone in the universe with no support or guidance. But the ancient mystics knew better. There's a reason why phrases like "Mother," "Father" and "Creator" are so prevalent in religious texts. Because there *is* a mother, a father and creator all rolled into one. There is a Home.

Think of it using the analogy of taking your child to preschool for the first time. Imagine that we were brought here by our mother and father and left here to educate ourselves, just like that terrifying first day of preschool might be for a three year-old. As a parent, you wouldn't leave your child at school without making sure the teachers had your phone number and were capable of caring for your child. You would not just abandon your child and leave her there with no support. You would make sure the child knows that somebody is always nearby, looking out for her safety, security and education.

That's what our mother/father/creator did when we decided to come to earth school. And that loving energy is watching over us all the time, sending signs, symbols and experiences to help us learn and grow. Imagine how much more comfortable we would be here on earth if we knew we could pick up a phone and call Home? Instead of a cell phone, we have a *soul* phone.

This is what the deepest ancient religious teachings have been trying to tell us. We *can* call home. And when we call, we can ask for guidance and receive answers. Our cosmic parents are always nearby, lovingly helping us to learn the ropes, heal our wounds and expand our awareness. We come to earth school for 8 seconds or 80 years, and when we're done we go Home, like coming home after a hard day at the office, whether we go home as a stillborn infant or as an old woman who's lived a long life.

From the perspective of Heaven, one person's experience is no more successful or tragic than another's. In this view, the ego dissolves, and all that remains is the light of soul, which only wants one thing... expansion and experience. When we look at earthly life from this vantage point, there can be nothing but love, because no other energy is supported at that level. From the Heaven view, we understand the purpose of tragedy. We understand that coming to earth with illness and poverty is the perfect combination of tools from the cosmic tool box. From the soul's point of view, a tragic loss is just what the doctor ordered, and from this place, all emotional and spiritual pain can be healed.

PLANNING OUR INCARNATIONS IS LIKE WRITING A MOVIE SCRIPT

The choice to incarnate is an enormous commitment for a soul because the soul knows that the ego will not recognize the soul's pre-birth agreements. For example, your soul might have designed a set of circumstances in which to be born where your parents are homeless drug addicts and the family lives a life of misery and despair. The soul -- and all the souls who are part of your family -- rejoice in the manifestation of that plan, because it will move the whole group forward in its spiritual evolution. But once incarnated, your ego/personality rails against those circumstances, and rightly so, because it's no fun living in misery and despair. You (your physical persona on earth) basically have three choices in how to deal with every pivotal experience:

1. You recognize that your soul created this experience as part of your educational curriculum on earth, so you embrace it with love, acceptance and gratitude.

2. You recognize the plan, but your ego is afraid of it, so you choose to stay in a safety zone and not receive those lessons right now. You can deal with it later, perhaps when you feel stronger, more financially secure or more loved. You can even choose to postpone those lessons for a future incarnation.

3. You conclude that the world is unfair, everybody is against you, there is no God and you are powerless.

The beauty of these choices is that they represent *exactly* what the soul came here to learn. Our experience on earth is a series of opportunities to take a higher view of every situation. The higher the perspective, the more peace we find in our lives. Finding our way through this maze is the whole point. It *is* the journey.

> "When we die, we carry the 'scars' from traumatic earth experiences to Heaven with us, because these experiences are vital to the work of our souls. Once in Heaven we view these imprints without attachment, as if we are reading a novel full of interesting characters. We *identify* with the characters, but we are not emotionally attached to them. It's like writing a script for a movie.
>
> We create the characters and their stories, and we sympathize with them, feel their pain and care about the outcome, but we do it with a certain detachment, because our only goal is to produce a good movie. We continue writing the script, no matter how much difficulty the character is experiencing. From my view in Heaven for example, I look at my last incarnation and I say, 'here's what happened in the last episode of my soul's story... I had a life-threatening illness, I had a father who left me, I died as

a teenager and as a result of these experiences, many other souls were transformed and I contributed to a shift in the collective consciousness.' This is excellent script material!

In script writing there's a term called "character arc," which is the point in the story where the characters learn something from their experiences and change in some way for the better. Planning an incarnation is all about that character arc. So when I look at my last lifetime, I see imprints from the many traumatic moments I experienced, and it's interesting, not sad or upsetting, just interesting. There's no judgment on it at all. It's like cleaning your house and seeing cobwebs or dust, and you just clean it up without emotion. It has no emotional charge. In fact, it has great love, because you're lovingly cleaning your house. The same is true when you look at the scars you carry to Heaven. You say, "Look at that beautiful scar, what a beautiful, juicy, rich, substantial piece of work that was!"

SOUL GROUPS AND UNCONDITIONAL VOLUNTEERS

It is difficult, if not impossible, to understand the gifts of tragedy without first understanding the concept of soul groups and unconditional volunteers. One of my favorite examples is the story of Adam Walsh, a little boy who was abducted from a department store and murdered in 1981. His father John Walsh turned tragedy into transformation by using his son's abduction and death to help parents locate missing children via the creation of The National Center for Missing and Exploited Children. The success of this group led the senior Walsh to become the host of the television show *America's Most Wanted,* which solved hundreds of crimes. The "Code Adam" program for helping lost children in department stores was established in Adam's memory, as was the Adam Walsh Child Protection and Safety Act.

Based on the understanding that our souls have a specific purpose which is fulfilled by the experiences we have on earth, every death provides profound growth for those whose lives are changed by that death. In this sense, any death, no matter how tragic, has a purpose, and the ability to see that purpose helps us feel less victimized . The

Walsh family's story is a beautiful illustration of this, because Adam's death triggered a series of events that transformed the entire world. Souls like Adam's, which Danny calls "unconditional volunteers," often come here specifically to lead that type of group transformation. Adam and his parents fulfilled a sacred contract to help humanity shift its awareness.

Like Adam -- and like my own son -- sometimes a soul will incarnate specifically to sponsor the growth of another soul or a group of souls. Consider the story of John Halgrim,[13] a boy who died of cancer in 2007 at age 15 after making an extraordinary request of the Make A Wish Foundation. John's wish was to open an orphanage for children in Africa, but of course Make A Wish wasn't equipped to grant such a wish. Just like in a movie, a wealthy philanthropist heard John's' story and stepped up to fund the project. John's family now travels to Africa regularly to work at the orphanage.

John Halgrim's story illustrates how a soul's intention is powerful enough to create a physically disabled body to serve a specific purpose. In this case, the soul group included not only John's immediate circle of friends and family, but also the philanthropist and his circle, plus the children in the orphanage, everybody involved with the project and all their circles. That soul group now also includes you, simply because I've shared this story with you. The knowledge you've gained from the story has increased your awareness about how soul groups work, and that shifts the way you see the world. The energy of thought in a soul group is fueled so strongly by the energy of God/Source that it manifests the exact situations in which the group's plans will be brought to fruition. In the case of John Halgrim, his friends and family, whether or not they'd ever engaged in charitable work, had, on a soul level, some serious charitable plans for this lifetime, and John came to lead them in this work.

This is true of every tragic death. If you look at the deaths of your loved ones with a view that encompasses the changes experienced by the soul family as a result of those deaths, you can see the greater plan. If the first step toward opening a conduit to the Divine is to believe

---

[13] www.johnhalgrimorphanage.com

that prayers and thoughts are heard in the higher realms, then the second step is to see the plan in its widescreen view rather than in the ego's view, which sees only the emotional responses of the body and the personality.

There are holy beings like John Halgrim and Adam Walsh all around you. You may even have one in your own family. Listen to what their souls are telling you.

"Choosing to come to earth is a volunteer act. It is a *sacrifice*, because we have many other options... we can remain non-physical and blended into oneness, or we can experiment with other life forms. Those who choose to incarnate on earth are volunteering to work for the growth of the whole, like a soldier volunteers to go to war to protect and defend a country or a principle. Even the 'bad guys' on earth are volunteers, and they have a very specific job, as you often describe when you talk about Hitler (one of his jobs, in addition to helping certain soul groups accomplish a mass plan for expansion, was to serve as the standard by which all bad behavior would be judged). If you are to understand the idea of oneness, this is an important concept... that we all enlisted for this service, to come to earth, create experiences and further the collective consciousness.

Some of us volunteer to be children who die tragically to teach their loved ones about releasing, grieving, transforming, serving others and a number of other lessons, including learning how life continues beyond the physical. Some volunteer to be serial killers or evil dictators, and some volunteer to be mentally imbalanced, abusive, corrupt, or thousands of other possibilities. All the roles are necessary for character arc. Somebody has to play the role of the bad guy, the villain, the hero and the victim. All are necessary.

Because we function as one united body, everything works like spokes on a wheel. They are separate, but part of the whole, and all are needed to make the wheel go around. This is how it looks from the view in Heaven.

The great reward in learning to see things this way is that you eventually realize that it's impossible to judge anyone for the roles they play. To judge that person would be like judging a character in a book, who does nothing more that serve a particular role to move the story along. This is a great gift, because in order to move deeper into the light, we must relinquish judgment completely. This is the true meaning of forgiveness."

THE EVOLUTION OF FORGIVENESS

Forgiveness is probably the single most difficult concept for the ego to understand. We feel pressured to forgive all the time, by Jesus and other spiritual teachers, by pop psychology books and by our friends and loved ones. But we just can't seem to wrap our minds around the idea of forgiving the cheating spouse, the child molester, the abusive parent or the evil dictator. What does forgiveness really mean, and why is it so important in spiritual work, especially in regard to death and dying?

Most of us confuse forgiving with *condoning*. But true forgiveness is not just about looking at someone who's hurt you and saying, "I forgive you for hurting me and I release my attachment to all the pain you caused me." While that may sound like a good line, it's not what forgiveness really looks like, though it's what most people *think* it looks like. Because as long as you believe the other person has *caused* your pain, you've missed the point. Releasing your attachment to that pain is a good start, but it's only the beginning in a long process of *understanding* forgiveness.

There are four levels of understanding forgiveness:

1. **Condoning bad behavior** - "If I forgive the person who molested me as a child, that means I've accepted or condoned what he's done and it somehow gets him off the hook, so therefore I cannot forgive."

2. **Releasing attachment to the behavior** - "I release my attachment to all the bad experiences, memories and responses I've carried in my heart as a result of my interactions with this person. I no longer wish to carry this anger around with me."

3. **Un-judging** - "This person is exactly like me on a soul level and I release him completely to his path. We are both here as volunteers to further the consciousness of the whole, and his purpose on earth is as Divine and necessary as mine or anyone else's."

4. **Gratitude** - "I recognize this experience as part of my soul's growth plan. I can see that this plan manifested perfectly through this experience, and feel deep gratitude for the lessons I received."

Looking at these four levels, you can see that forgiveness actually *evolves* through a series of steps that move toward higher and higher consciousness.

At Level One you are still in separation mentality, where you see yourself and your experience as disconnected from the collective consciousness. At Level Two you move toward a more compassionate, non-attached perspective, but there is still separation as long as you feel that something has been "done" to you. At Level Three you begin to embrace oneness and see that every action has a purpose. At this level you can not only forgive and release, you can actually move to an even higher plane... *gratitude* (Level Four). At Level Four you see that all experience is a co-creation, and every experience is precious and perfect in its design for furthering the growth of individual souls and soul groups.

Using our favorite poster boy for evil, Adolf Hitler as an example, at Level One there are many wounded, bitter people on earth who refuse to forgive him because they think that forgiveness will excuse or condone his actions in some way. There is a powerful illusion at work here... the idea that withholding forgiveness constitutes some sort of punishment. As long as there's no forgiveness, punishment is being levied.

At Level Two we would start to see that we don't have to condone him or even *tolerate* him, but we can release our personal attachment to the experience. At Level Three the whole picture shifts because we can begin to see him as one of "us" instead of one of "them." And at Level Four, all of humanity can be seen from a higher perspective where the trauma of war and oppression is part of human evolution, and we're grateful for the growth lessons.

These are not steps in a process. They are *levels of perception.* As we learn and evolve, we will perceive events in different ways. This is part of the reason we design tragic events, so they can serve as opportunities to move us through that evolution and shift our perceptions to levels that bring us closer to oneness.

Whether we're talking about a traumatic childhood, a plane crash, a shooting on a high school campus or a village bombed in a war, soul groups are brought together for a common experience. At Levels Three and Four, the shooter at the high school is no different than the teenager who is shot, and the military officer who gives the order to bomb a village is no different than the victims in the village. The groups of souls that came together to share the experience agreed to meet in this location at this time for this event. Every event in the universe, traumatic or otherwise, creates a ripple effect that transmits a limitless array of transformative responses for each soul involved.

When a village is bombed in a war, each participant takes away something unique from that experience, and those participants include the people at ground level, the pilot flying the bomber, the commander who gave the order, the families of the dead, the survivors of the bombing (and their descendants), the people of the nations involved in the war, and people throughout the world who will be affected in some way by that war. The repercussions impact every aspect of human life... politics, technology, law, journalism, language, culture, religious ideals, social structures, art, literature, science and more. It even affects the animal, plant and mineral worlds. Because everything is connected, everything shifts.

Even if the shift is barely perceptible, each tiny movement contributes to the increased awareness of the collective. I often compare this to the turning of a kaleidoscope. With the tiniest movement, the fragments rearrange themselves and a new structure is created. We are as interconnected as those kaleidoscope fragments, and with this understanding, it's easy to see what the great spiritual teachers mean when they say that WE ARE ALL ONE.

This constantly changing perspective is exactly the kind of momentum our souls crave.

KARMA

When the Tibetan Buddhists first brought their teachings to the west in the 1950s, the word "karma" came along with them, and within two decades the word became part of American pop culture. You could see it everywhere from bumper stickers ("my karma ran over your dogma") to department stores ("shoplifting is bad karma").

Buddhist teachings arrived in the west as a direct result of the Chinese invasion of Tibet, when monasteries were burned and monks were forced into exile. This event was in itself a magnificent act of karma, because as the monks traveled through the world, their teachings eventually landed on the shores of Europe and America, and brought waves of new spiritual understanding to western minds. This is an excellent example of how tragedy fuels the growth of the whole. There was a growth plan for the monks as well as the westerners, because the monks, after centuries of seclusion, needed to have a uniquely human experience (war, invasion, exile) in order to truly practice compassion by releasing judgment against their oppressors. Before they came into the world to share their sacred teachings, they had to experience their own humanity so they could understand the human condition.

But we westerners could not wrap our minds around the concept of karma. How could we? Our thinking is so locked into biblical notions of judgment and punishment that we instinctively apply those notions to the concept of karma. We westernize it to fit our values, just as we westernize reincarnation. We turn those ideas into systems of reward and punishment ruled by a judgmental entity, when in fact karma contains no judgment at all. Remember what Matthew said in Chapter Two about the warrior who kills an enemy and in another lifetime the two willingly switch places to allow both an opportunity to achieve balance? Buddhists understand balance. But westerners think in terms of payback. There's a big difference.

There is no payback because there is no payer or payee. Karma is simply the law of cause and effect, and like God, it does not judge us. It simply refers to the effect of every action on every other action. The only karma involved in shoplifting is that you'll either get a nice new sweater for free or you'll go to jail. Do you have to pay back the universe for the stolen sweater in a future incarnation? No. Will you go to jail for stealing the sweater? Maybe. Going to jail for breaking a law is justice, but karma isn't about justice. It's about *balance.* If you steal a sweater because you're homeless and cold and need it to survive, you won't have to reincarnate as a thief who gets his hand cut off for stealing. But if you've made a career of stealing from others, then your soul will *choose* to experience the other side of those events in order to get a well-rounded, balanced human experience.

Balancing is a *choice.* A soul can choose to balance the karma of a lifetime as a criminal by designing an incarnation in which he will be the victim of similar crimes. But it's a choice made by the soul for growth, not a punishment imposed on us by a higher power. We *are* the higher power. The only one judging us is *us.* There *is* nobody else.

We can also choose not to balance our karma, at least not right away. Hitler may return to earth as a benevolent, compassionate man with a comfortable life, and he may choose that for a thousand lifetimes rather than choose a prison camp experience to balance the energy. But as his soul evolves and he seeks to work with those energies, he will eventually move toward balancing his experience. This is true for everybody. If you signed up for a particular curriculum, perhaps to work on being a healer, you will eventually design a course of study that includes all the various aspects of the healer energy -- including the experience of illness, disability or discord.

There are millions of scenarios that can illustrate how karma is created and balanced. For example, if your friend is killed in a gang shooting you might respond by retaliating and shooting a rival gang member, which brings yet another soul group -- and all its branches -- into the story. Or you might respond by becoming a social worker who influences kids not to join gangs. Or you might spiral into drug use, depression or suicide, or you might run for office on a gun control platform and become the next mayor of your city.

Karma refers to the kaleidoscope effect of all experience, where each action by one of us will affect the rest of us. This doesn't mean that the gang member who did the shooting has to get shot by someone else to even the score, or that he was murdered by someone in a past life and is now paying it back in this one. It's never about payback. It's about creating actions that fulfill a growth request made by the souls involved.

At the writing of this book in Spring 2009, the economy of the United States was in shambles. Millions of people -- myself included -- lost their incomes and had their houses foreclosed while the corruption in corporate America was exposed for all to see. While I struggled with my financial losses, I also recognized that this soul group experience was an opportunity for mass transformation. The economic crash affected every person in exactly the area where they needed the most growth. For me it was about moving from working as an hourly marketing/copywriting contractor to focusing exclusively on my true work as an author and spiritual teacher. Of the millions who lost their jobs, some resigned themselves to blame and bitterness while others saw it as a chance to pursue their entrepreneurial dreams, spend more time with their families or change their shopping habits. This is group karma at its finest, rippling through the entire world in search of large-scale transformation and an elevated perspective. During this time in America, military enlistment went up and president Obama worked to end the war in Iraq. In my fantasy, millions of educated, skilled workers would join the military because there were no jobs anywhere else, and as a result, without a war burning through billions of dollars each day, the military would be transformed into an organization focused on humanitarian service.

OK, that may be a little far-fetched. But the point is that all souls work together, whether they know it or not. And our souls ultimately win the battle with our egos, whether we like it or not. Our egos hate it when we lose our jobs, but our souls know that something better waits around the corner. The more we become aware of how this works, the faster the growth occurs in our individual lives and in our soul groups.

While living in the density of the earth plane it's difficult to recognize ourselves as Divine beings. Many teachers have come to earth to remind us what we are and where we come from, but they're usually laughed at, ignored or murdered. Jesus is a perfect example. He was as an unconditional volunteer too.

ANIMALS AS UNCONDITIONAL VOLUNTEERS

Last summer a friend came to visit me who was very excited about attending my town's annual rodeo. She persuaded me to go with her, and I did. It was the first time I'd been to a rodeo, and it will definitely be the last.

The show opened with cowboys chasing and harnessing "wild" horses. I began to sob at that point, and by the time they got around to calf roping I was so distressed I had to leave. I could feel the souls of those animals (no, I am not a vegetarian) and I could also hear my guides trying to comfort me. This is what they said:

"All living beings; plants, animals, humans and even minerals, have agreements about the roles they will play during the life span of this planet. The animals are aware of the agreement and have no reason to violate it, because they have no egos prompting them to change or violate the agreement. They are not on earth to accumulate experience the way humans are, so they don't have the need to experience the pain of separation. They *know* they are not separate, and don't have any reason to create a separation experience. But the abuse or exploitation of animals disrespects this sacred contract and creates a very dark, imbalanced energy. This is what you were sensing at the rodeo. You cried for the dishonoring of the agreement."

My guides taught me that the souls of animals are different because they are here as teachers, companions and supporters, serving us in the same way angels serve us. They're not separate from Heaven at all, because they didn't need to create the *idea* of separation like humans did. In pondering this, I realized that learning about animal souls is part of my work in helping people deal with grief, because many are grieving for their pets.

I was once told by my guides that angels function like fireflies... they are carriers of the light, and their job is to keep the conduits and energy channels between dimensions clean and clear. Part of that task involves watching over us to help us attain our souls' intentions, because the more aligned we are with those intentions, the cleaner the conduits are and the more love can pass between worlds. That is what the angels are here to do, and animals are very similar to this.

The animals know they are part of the whole, which is why, on a soul level, they have agreed to serve as food, materials, labor and sacrifices for religious rituals. Death doesn't mean the same thing to them that it does to humans, because they understand that they will blend into the oneness after honoring their agreements on earth. They don't need to reincarnate, but their souls, which are similar to the energy of angels, happily choose to serve on earth. All the experiences animals have, including abuse and mistreatment, are part of the package. The violence of prey and predator is expected and honored among the animals in natural life. And even when animals live with abusive humans, part of that plan is to give other humans who become aware of the abuse an opportunity to learn about our sacred contracts with animals.

For animals, not only is there no separation, they represent oneness to humans in everything they do. We eat them and they become part of our bodies. Their excrement fertilizes our soil. They till our land, carry us from place to place, make themselves available for ancient religious rituals and modern scientific experimentation, and provide love as pets and companions. On a soul level, they are selfless servants who act as connective tissue to hold the human experience together (though of course we are ALL part of this connective tissue).

Animals are like the guides and angels who hover nearby to humans, jumping up and down waving their hands trying to get our attention to say, "Please look and see what we're here for so you can understand what we're *all* here for." They are representatives of the wholeness.

FORGETTING HEAVEN

One of the many experiences we have in Heaven involves remembering how to detach from the worry and fear that obsessed us on earth. It's like learning how to play as a child does, free from adult worries and feeling completely secure and protected. There is a specific purpose in Heaven for experiencing this feeling, because it is part of preparing for our return to earth.

Because we come in as newborn babies and must live through babyhood and childhood, we can't come in with the weight of all our lifetimes cluttering up our memories. We have to arrive on earth with *trust,* so part of the preparation for coming back to earth is a process my guides call "joy lessons."

During these lessons our teachers in the higher realms help us release the heaviness and pain of our accumulated incarnations. They strip away memories and imprints so that we can become childlike in preparation for birth. Danny, who loves using movies to illustrate spiritual truths, says that the process is similar to what took place in the movie *Men in Black* when they erased people's memories of encounters with aliens. Most of our memory of Heaven is erased, and with it, the memory of the work we've done in our past lives, thus restoring an open, childlike mind.

It has to be that way. Imagine what it would be like to come to earth with clear memories of living completely on the soul level with all the information in the Akashic records in our minds. What would a five year-old be like with all that data in her consciousness?

There are actually plenty of children like this on earth; psychic children, gifted prodigies, Indigos, Crystals and many others. Often this is the case with depressed, disabled or "retarded" children. There are holes in the mesh, and the memories of other realms come through. But it's not because the cleansing process didn't work. It's because these souls *chose* to retain this knowledge as part of their plan for that life. So the soul of a psychic child or a child with Down Syndrome brings a piece of Heaven back to earth to share with others. It is just as likely that the drunk homeless man muttering about God as he stumbles through the city streets is also such a soul. Souls like this can take the form of gifted children or psychotics, but either way, they are sacred teachers.

We don't remember Heaven because in order to learn the lessons we've chosen via incarnation, a certain amount of separation is necessary. To see something clearly you have to step back from it a bit. You can't see a picture if it's held right up against your face. Separation from the oneness is necessary in order to gain human experience, and human experience is all about finding our way back to oneness. It's a game that our souls love to play for the same reason that kids like to go into those scary fun houses in amusement parks. They scream and get scared, but they know when it's over they'll come back out into the light, back home to familiarity and safety.

"When we make the choice to live on earth, an energetic process happens in which we move energy through the frequencies in order to densify enough to manifest physical bodies. There's so much energy that it can't help but tighten and compress enough to create matter. All of physical life is a result of this compression. And in contrast to the compression, there is expansion, and the expansion is what our souls do when they learn and grow. Coming to earth is the compression, and raising our frequencies to reconnect with Heaven is the expansion. It is a natural law, these two motions.

If you compress enough... BOOM! You become matter. And because matter requires so much compression and density to manifest, it naturally creates resistance to the higher, lighter frequencies. This energy has a life force of its own, and the souls of all living things in the physical realm have agreed to be part of this process, coming in and out of density in different forms. Once we understand how this system works, we can ultimately choose physical life or not.

In physical life we forget these things because our perception of time on earth is linear. But when time is all happening simultaneously -- all events at the same time -- there is an infinite well of information that we can tap into, and from this well we can extract whatever material we choose, including images from the future. The future images are fuzzy because they're only possibilities; they are images inserted into creation plans, but those plans are always subject to change. All the experiences and lessons are there for the taking, and they'll be activated at one point or another in your soul's journey, including every death, every birth, every relationship and every experience. The soul recognizes how these events fit into its plan and will choose which to activate during which incarnation.

All of creation is part of our soul family, but members come in and out to work directly with one another at different times. Perhaps we incarnate together as friends or family members, or perhaps we work together across dimensions. Either way, we work as one connected organism in which each part, each cell, each element and each breath is part of the whole."

HOW BIRTH HAPPENS

What you just read in the paragraphs above is pretty typical of the information I receive from Danny and my guides on the Other Side. They are eloquent, thoughtful, gentle teachers who delight in any opportunity to share their wisdom. Sometimes their explanations are scientific (or at least what I'd consider scientific, though the scientific community would laugh uproariously at all this). And at other times their explanations are magical, based on an uncommon reality where the physical and the non-physical overlap. One of the sweetest conversations we ever had was when they explained the birds and the bees to me in a way that only Divine, discarnate parents could:

"Imagine it is the beginning of human time as you know it, and we are still pure spirit having a collective thought about coming to earth. The energy of that thought is powerful enough to create matter, which would give us physical bodies, but in order to get ourselves in to those bodies, we have to create a system that moves us between dimensions. We had to design human forms that we could inhabit, and then we had to figure out how to place ourselves inside those forms.

It's as if an ancient team of planners organized a mass exodus of souls into bodies as a sort of field trip, a science experiment if you will. As if a high school science teacher said to her students, 'Let's pick a planet and experience what life is like there. In order to learn while we're on this planet, we'll have to experience everything possible that comes with life in that realm. So let's design a vehicle in which to have these experiences.' And a rough design for the human body was conjured up. The perfect housing for a soul on an archeological expedition to earth!

The next step in the planning process is to develop a transport system for delivering souls into those bodies. Suddenly, somebody sitting around the cosmic conference table has a brainstorm.

'I know!' he says. 'The returning souls can come to earth through the existing bodies!'

Everybody high-fives each other as they recognize the brilliance of this plan. What better place to build a body than inside an existing one? The reproductive process is then fine-tuned, and voila! We have an interdimensional transport system. We are the designers, in partnership with the energy known as God. It's a joint venture. This is the true meaning of intelligent design.

When a baby is born it has a bewildered look on its face. The blinking eyes express a mix of awe and confusion, and knowing this story, you can imagine what that soul is experiencing. The babies are saying, "blink, blink, what just happened?" Their souls know exactly what happened, but in order to live on earth, the memory of the soul's knowledge has to move into the background, so babies are completely stunned by the ego field at birth. They've just arrived on a commuter train called a mother's body. What a system!"

SOUL MATES

Just like the concept of karma, the concept of soul mates has been commercialized and romanticized to the detriment of us all. The truth is that we do not have one specific soul mate, on earth or anywhere else.

Instead, we have many, many soul family members who work with us in different roles through our various incarnations. Our soul mates are the ones who have the most profound impact, the most influence and the strongest emotional connection, but they are not limited to lovers and spouses. They can include our children, pets, best friends or beloved college professors. A soul mate does not necessarily show up in your life to provide a happy romantic relationship that lasts forever. He or she can just as likely be someone who provides a lifetime of abuse, neglect or indifference.

> "Even in a perceived state of conflict there is harmony. The personality may perceive that partners are in conflict, but from the view of the soul, the partners are acting out the exact lessons they came to earth to experience. In this sense they're working in perfect harmony. Harmony doesn't necessarily mean a lack of friction. It means being aligned with the soul's intention."

Here's a quick formula for figuring out who's a soul mate and who isn't. If this person came into your life to help move you toward the lessons your soul signed on for, then he or she is a soul mate. It is just as likely to be the beloved spouse you lived happily with for 50 years as the drunk driver who sideswiped your car and left you paralyzed.

Several months ago I listened to a CD that contained a guided meditation for finding a soul mate,[14] and it gave an excellent explanation of how souls find one another. In this meditation, you visualize your soul broadcasting its energy out into the universe in search of a resonant energy... the energy of another soul that is magnetically drawn to your own. In doing this meditation you are

---

[14] Sanaya Roman, "Attracting Your Soul Mate."

literally sending out a beacon of soul light that bears the message, "I'm here. Come find me." And somewhere, someone else is sending out a similar request. The two energies reach across the universe until they link up at a critical meeting point where the work of the two souls will continue in physical form. But the messages don't necessarily have to be beamed out consciously via a guided meditation CD. We're broadcasting our requests all the time, whether we're aware of it or not. The energies will always find one another, and will always end up in the right place at the right time. There are no wrong people, wrong energies or wrong times.

This is how soul family members find one another, and this process takes place 24/7, though most of us are not aware of it. We're constantly broadcasting subconscious messages that create the people, events and experiences that appear in our lives. If one broadcasts a message of negativity, abandonment and lack, this is what will be created. One we learn how the creation process works, we can broadcast more specifically and intentionally exactly what we want to create. That's what the laws of attraction are all about. But what popular culture missed when it latched on to the law of attraction is that we are not only supposed to create the easy, happy, safe experiences. We also need to create difficult, challenging events to fuel our growth. That's the secret that *The Secret* neglected to tell us.

Most of us aren't spiritually fine-tuned enough to be fully aware of what we're publishing on our psychic printing presses. Most of the time we're mindlessly broadcasting a chaotic mix of past experiences, limiting beliefs, wounds, fears, traumas, fantasies and flotsam from our many incarnations. But at a certain point in the soul's education one learns that these images and broadcasts can be commanded and structured to serve a higher authority... the soul rather than the ego.

Despite what we see in movies, meeting our mates is never just a cute, quirky coincidence. What may look like a charming romantic comedy on the outside is really a recognition and reconnection of energies that agreed to share a particular learning experience. Not terribly romantic, but romance is fleeting, and soul mates are forever, whether or not the two personalities stay together in the physical world. As the Course in Miracles says, there are no special relationships. We are all soul mates because we are all interconnected.

Many of the newly-widowed people I've worked with wonder if the deceased spouse will be jealous when a new partner enters the picture. From the soul's perspective, the mate in Heaven could no more be jealous of a new partner than be jealous of his own Self. Because in order to have jealousy, blame or even forgiveness, there must be separateness. In order to step aside and feel such feelings, there has to be an "other." On the Heaven plane, it becomes clear that there is no "other," because we are all one and there is no separation. As the Course in Miracles says, "There is only one of us here."

When we can learn to recognize every person as a partner who delivers teaching tools and gifts of growth, our hearts can begin to open to oneness. And when that opening occurs, we can experience life on earth with wonder rather than fear, curiosity rather than resistance, and gratitude rather than hopelessness.

FREE WILL

Your free will is at the forefront of everything you do. Free will is a tool; a gift we are granted as part of our incarnate experience (incarnation would be impossible without free will). Of course you are always being guided and directed by Spirit, which includes the connective energy of God, the angels, guides and your higher self, but your free will allows you to make the choices that will lead you to this path or that, which will lead you to this lesson or that. It is your free will that chooses to write a book, to choose a partner or drive to the grocery store. Even though you are being assisted by your invisible helpers, you are doing the actual physical task. Your guides cannot make decisions for you. They can only guide you to the feast of possibilities that are available. So in this sense you *are* working alone, at the moment of decision. Your free will is also the mechanism that allows you to choose to heed Divine guidance or not. How many on earth resist Divine guidance in their lives? They see the signs, the alleged "coincidences" and "accidents," and choose not to interpret them as messages from guides. That is an act of free will. Those of us on a spiritual path can make a different choice… to listen and heed what is presented. It's the true meaning of "active listening."

4. Family Ties

In keeping with the idea of soul mates and soul families, this chapter delves more deeply into pre-birth contracts, volunteer agreements and the ways in which everything works interdependently by looking at how our life plans are packaged into scenarios that teach us specific lessons on earth. I've used several examples from my own life, and quote my guides rather extensively here, because they've answered my questions with such clarity when I've asked about why certain situations happened the way they did.

I'd like to start by sharing some stories from a children's grief recovery camp where I volunteered for two summers. The weekend camp is run by our local hospice and is offered free of charge to children in the community who've experienced the death of a loved one. Volunteers are specially trained to be compassionate listeners for the children, because many of the kids never had the chance to talk openly about their experiences.

Many of those experiences were incomprehensibly dreadful. A surprisingly large percentage of the kids had experienced the suicide of a parent, and because of the family's shame, horror and denial, were discouraged from asking questions or talking about the event. One eight year-old told me that when his mother died mysteriously, nobody in his family would give him any information about what happened. Being an inquisitive and assertive child, he went door-to-door in his neighborhood asking people if they could tell him what happened to his mother. I don't know how he eventually figured out that it was a suicide, but thankfully, someone in his family was wise enough to send him to our camp, where he got some much-needed support.

Some of the deaths I've heard about at camp are less controversial, such as car wrecks or illnesses, but in every situation, the children benefit tremendously from spending time with other kids who've had similar experiences. They also respond beautifully to the rituals and processes we do throughout the weekend to help them deal with their grief. On Saturday afternoon we set up an arts & crafts area so the kids can make "memory boats" out of large pieces of bark from the local trees (donated by the local loggers). They decorate the bark boats with moss, twigs, flowers, feathers and scraps of paper on which they write messages to their loved ones. On Sunday morning we go to the river and set the little boats adrift as a visual expression of releasing and letting go. Some of the kids run alongside the river following their boats as far as they can, and others simply stand still, watching the boats disappear around the bend. This, and other rituals like it, gives the kids an outlet for expressing their pain by creating physical objects, movements and symbols that bring their feelings from a wordless, lonely world into tangible physical reality.

Another boy I met -- I'll call him Jacob -- was 11 years old when he first came to camp, even though his mother's suicide had occurred six years earlier. Jacob was exceptionally bright and surprisingly open about his experiences. He told me that he wanted to be a grief counselor when he grew up, and that he'd already become involved as a peer counselor in a grief recovery group organized by his school. As Jacob and I bonded over the weekend, he revealed bits and pieces of his story. When he was five years old, he slept on a cot in his mother's bedroom. One night while sleeping, he heard a loud noise that woke him up. He looked across the dark room to where his mother slept in her bed and thought it was odd that she had ketchup on her head, but he didn't think much of it and soon went back to sleep. When he woke up in the morning he discovered that she'd shot herself in the head.

After he told me this story, I went into the woods, where I wailed and cried for ten minutes before I could return to camp with some semblance of composure. I could not in a thousand lifetimes understand why a mother would do such a thing to a child. I realized that my own grief experiences were a walk in the park compared to this. What was lesson here? What kind of agreement did the souls of Jacob and his mother have?

"It isn't just an agreement between Jacob and his mother. It is an agreement between a large soul group of which these two were members, and also touches the many souls Jacob will work with as a grief counselor in the future. The mother had been tormented for many lifetimes and this was not her first suicide.

Jacob has been her friend, lover, father, mother and caregiver through many incarnations, and has felt responsible for her. Her gift to him with this suicide, as difficult as it may be to see this event as a gift, was to release him from being so deeply enmeshed in the caregiver role with her so that he could carry the caregiving energy forward as a teacher and counselor for others. In this lifetime Jacob is working through learning that he cannot change the plan of another soul. He has done this dance with his mother's soul many times. They have decided together that she would end this cycle in a dramatic way, though he is now also a caregiver to his father, friends and family members and continues to work with the caregiver energy. What he will learn here is a final understanding that he is not in charge or responsible for another's choices. This is a lesson his soul has chosen. There is no easy or painless way to learn this lesson."

MY METAPHYSICAL FAMILY TREE

Although I believe in reincarnation (a curriculum of cosmic learning would not be possible without it), I've never been as interested in the details of my past lives as some people are. I know dozens of mediums, channelers and psychics who do past life readings for their clients, complete with intimate details of relationships, causes of death, locations, periods in history and even names. While these details are interesting, they're not always necessary, because all that matters is the *energy* we're working with from one lifetime to the next. So for Jacob to work with the energy of caregiving, he would incarnate in a number of different scenarios to bring that energy forward. In ancient Egypt he might have worked in the healing arts as part of his training as a caregiver. And in 20th century England he might have been a female prostitute, which would give him the experience of female powerlessness and despair. You can see how these experiences would fit into the work he's doing in this lifetime with his mother.

To best illustrate this, I'm going to share an intimate piece of my personal history, because it reveals how deep the patterns of interconnectedness between souls can be. Most of this information was channeled via Danny and my other guides, so the best way I can

63

express it is to use their words exactly as I received them. But in order to understand this, it's necessary to give you some background information.

When I was a young woman I had three unplanned pregnancies. I terminated the first two, and the third was a life threatening ectopic pregnancy that resulted in the removal of one of my fallopian tubes. Since I was certain that I never wanted children and didn't want another unwanted pregnancy, I asked the doctor to "tie" the remaining tube while he was doing the surgery to remove the damaged one.

Fast forward a decade or so and I have now married Jim, a stable, devoted man who wanted children more than anything in the world. We spent a couple of years trying various fertilization technologies that all failed, and eventually we ended up adopting Danny. Danny's birth mother was a lovely young woman named Erika, and Erika's mother -- Danny's biological grandmother -- was Paula, who died when Danny was two years old (and now appears frequently in my meditations). Four years later Jim and I divorced, and a few years after that Danny was diagnosed with the disease that ended his physical life.

The disease was *genetic*.

Although we were divorced, Jim stayed quite close to us and was an attentive, supportive father before Danny's illness. But after Danny got sick, Jim slowly faded from Danny's life, feeling that caregiving and the emotional burden of a dying child was too much for him to bear. I was curious about why Jim would write a disabled, dying child into his life plan and then choose not to receive the lessons offered in that scenario. Of course I was quickly corrected by my guides about my interpretation of this. Jim received the exact lessons his soul needed for its current evolutionary status, and his curriculum tied in perfectly to everybody else's. If Jim had stayed involved in Danny's life, the pieces in the kaleidoscope would have shifted into a different pattern. The pattern we had to work with was designed precisely to further the growth of our collective souls.

My guides have explained to me that Jim, Erika, Paula and the other players in this story were part of an agreement to bring Danny in as my son, which was part of a plan to usher me toward my current work as a spiritual teacher. This plan was also designed to move

Danny forward as a healer in the higher realms, which is the work he has chosen, and is an inextricable part of *my* work. Danny's relationship with Jim was also part of this work, because the experience of abandonment is now part of Danny's knowledge base, which he uses to help others. The focus of Danny's work as a teacher in Heaven is to help people see Heaven through human relationships.

A network of family ties that includes past lives and pre-birth agreements gives a whole new meaning to the concept of six degrees of separation. Because the branches are so far-reaching and the roots go so deep, and because soul groups ultimately include everybody in the universe, it's impossible to trace a complete family tree. The bottom line is that we're all in this together. We're all connected.

Those of you who've read my previous book may remember how I met a guide named Arlen during a meditation. I was told that he serves as a teacher to Danny in Heaven and has been incarnated with both Danny and me in several lifetimes. I never had any details about those lifetimes because I never felt the need to ask, but one day those details came to me quite by surprise via this unexpected dialog with Danny about our family ties:

ME: Was that *you* in my pregnancies? Were you trying to come through and I rejected you?

DANNY: Yes, but I didn't come through then because it wasn't the right time for my birth. The termination of those pregnancies and the ectopic pregnancy that resulted in sterilization created physical and emotional conditions that eventually lead you to adoption. And through adoption we were able to get the genetic defect that caused my illness. Those events were necessary to create the right circumstances for our life plan, and those circumstances were a *result* of the pregnancies. The genetic code from my birth mother Erika produced my illness and my death, which was a huge growth step for all of us. Adoption also brought Erika's mother Paula into our lives, who has been a spirit guide to you for many lifetimes. Everything needed to be in place for this phase of our work to begin, so the pregnancies were necessary to create the right circumstances. It is that way in every life. Everything happens for a very specific reason.

ME: Why is Paula one of my guides? I feel her presence all the time.

DANNY: Ah, beautiful Paula, she is a source of goddess/mother energy to both of us. In fact, she has been just that, our mother, in past lives.

I am giving you a vision right now of all of us in an ancient, sun-baked land. It is Rome, where you are a daughter to Paula and I am your little brother. Arlen is also there, and he is a constant presence in our life, always in our house, but he is not Paula's husband. Paula's husband, our father, has died. Arlen tends the land, like a caretaker. He has always been a caretaker for our family, much like he is now from the higher realms.

We lived in comfort, not really wealth, but certainly in the upper classes. Paula's husband left her wealth and property. We lived in peace, and there was music, art and joy in our lives. Arlen was our teacher, but because he was poor, like a slave or a serf, he could not be recognized as a teacher (most great teachers create a life of poverty). His wealth comes from the soul, and he is loved by many people. You and I often played in the garden with him, which is why you first saw him in your meditations up in a tree picking fruit. This is actually a past life memory of Arlen in a tree, working. This is how your soul remembers him from this particular incarnation. Paula lived a good life and died an old woman. There was a lot of peace and comfort in this lifetime.

ME: I'm getting the sense that Arlen went away after a while. He died?

DANNY: He died in an accident in a field. He fell out of a tree.

ME: C'mon, you're kidding me! Is that a joke?

DANNY: You don't believe that do you? You think you're making it up rather than hearing it from me. This is an excellent exercise in channeling. Why did you see him in a tree in your first vision? Why would it not be possible that all this ties together? His death left a huge impression on you. You were a young girl. You were in love with him, but he was older. It was a little girl crush. It many ways this affected your lifelong pattern of loss with men.

ME: He is my original father figure?

DANNY: Yes, and your first love. Remember, our father had died. So you lost him, then Arlen. You were 12 when Arlen died. You and I were like any typical brother and sister, playing in the garden dirt, teasing each other. You followed Arlen around everywhere, like a puppy. He taught you about gardening and land, which is why you love it so much now.

ME: What happened to you? I'm getting the impression that you went away too. To a war or something. I lost you too?

DANNY: I did go to war for a short time, and traveled far away. I was a man, and this is what men did. I went off to earn a living, sometimes as a solider, sometimes a laborer, a jack of all trades, always traveling. I became enamored of the other cultures I visited and stayed to study wherever I went. I became a teacher, much like Arlen. He guided me from Heaven.

ME: So I was left all alone?

DANNY: You weren't alone. You had Paula. You took care of her until she died. This is part of the reason she takes care of you now.

ME: And then she died too! My big loss story!

DANNY: Yes, it is your big loss story. This is why you are teaching people to cope with grief and loss now. You teach people to look at loss with new eyes. How could you teach this if you hadn't spent lifetimes learning to see it differently? That is your true gift. You are teaching people how to understand death and loss with a more enlightened perspective. It is that simple.

ME: So now what? Am I going to have these intense losses over and over again in this lifetime?

DANNY: You will have the same losses that all people have, because it is important for you to understand their losses in order to help them. The difference is that you will see the losses differently. They will not traumatize you like they do others. And you will be able to help others find a new way to understand these experiences. Part of your plan for this incarnation was to receive Divine input. You prayed for this since you were a teenager, and every event in your life has supported that prayer. In order to know God, your heart had to be open, and in order for it to open, you had to know God. It's a cosmic Catch 22. Pain contributes to the flexibility of the heart, and without it you would not recognize the jeweled lessons you are receiving. You have asked to work closely with the guides, and in order to do this, your heart must be flexible. This is a true commitment to God, because it is painful to have an open heart, as you have learned. But it is also the most direct route to receiving from the Divine.

I was utterly surprised to receive this much information about a past life without even asking for it, and I marveled at how much sense it made. It's true that I can never look at anything the same way again, not just as a result of Danny's death, but as a result of the amazing perspective I've been given in regard to all the losses I've had through my various lifetimes. The learning curve is obvious.

The story I just told about this past life with Danny involved soul family members who incarnated together frequently. By contrast, I now want to share a story about how a group of strangers can also serve each other's growth. In this case, these strangers became a vital part of my work as a metaphysical grief counselor. It's a great example of how deep our soul connections and patterns of perfection can go.

One day my friend Harold -- a man in his 80s -- gifted me with an old book called "Invisible Helpers," which he'd unearthed while cleaning out his attic. Harold knows my spiritual proclivities, and knew the book was meant for me. It was published by the Theosophical Society in 1912 (they're big on after-death communication) and written by C. W. Leadbeater. I read most of it with great interest, and then added it to the pile of unfinished books on my bedside table with a bookmark at the end of chapter nine.

Around this time I got a postcard in the mail from the General Motors Corporation informing me of a recall on a part of the car I'd recently purchased. I had to bring the car to a dealership in the next town to have the part replaced, so I asked my friend Kelsey to meet me there and drive me home after I dropped off my car.

After turning my car over the mechanics and the dealership, Kelsey called my cell phone to tell me she was running late, so I went to the reception area to wait for her. In the reception area was a television tuned to a local news channel, and I entered the room just in time to see a news segment about a 5 year-old boy who'd hit his head on a rock while playing in a rock quarry with his older brother. I was mesmerized by the story and felt intense pain for the family, especially for the brother who would probably struggle with guilt for the rest of his life. I said a silent prayer to my guides, especially to Danny, asking them to stand with this family and help them. They instantly gave me an image of the boy arriving in Heaven, and I heard Danny say, "He is a member of our soul family. Don't worry. We've got him."

A couple of important points to note here. I do not have local TV channels on my cable system, and as long as I've lived in this area I've never seen the local news. I would not have seen that report if I hadn't gone to the car dealership that day and if Kelsey had been on time. There was clearly a reason for me to see that story.

For the next few days all I could think about was those two brothers. I felt the dead boy's presence around me constantly, and I even made some calls to people in our community who knew the family, and offered to help in any way I could. I was assured that the family had a strong church network and had all the spiritual help they needed. I knew there was nothing I could do -- in the physical world -- to help them.

A few nights later I lay in my bed unable to sleep, feeling agitated and obsessed about this family. I Noticed *The Invisible Helpers* on the bedside table and thought that reading might help put me to sleep. I opened the book to where I'd left the bookmark at the end of Chapter nine and turned the page to the beginning of Chapter 10. The name of the chapter was *The Two Brothers*.

The chapter was about two brothers who lived in 1897 Scotland -- Walter and Lancelot. They were out riding horses together when Lancelot fell off his horse, hit his head on a rock and died. Walter was destroyed by grief and guilt, wouldn't eat or leave his bed, and his parents thought he was dying of a broken heart. In this story, the spirit of Lancelot stood by Walter's side the whole time, but Walter was too grief stricken and emotional to see it. So Lancelot asked his guides to help him manifest a visual image of himself for Walter to see, so that Walter would be comforted and assured that Lancelot was not really gone.

I knew this story had come to me on this particular day for a reason. It didn't come last week or last month when I'd started reading the book. It came *today,* after a week of agonizing about the boy who died in the rock quarry. But why? What was the connection? How was this boy part of my soul family?

"The magnificent timing of these events -- the boy's death, your trip to the car dealership and the reading of Chapter 10 in the book -- is part of a powerful teaching your soul has requested. You have felt confident about offering healing and guidance to parents who've lost a child to illness, but have felt inadequate to help parents who've experienced a child's sudden, seemingly preventable death. You have asked, from the depth of your soul, for teaching tools to help you address this topic with confidence, and we -- *your* invisible helpers -- led you to this experience to help expand your understanding.

You would not have heard the news if you'd not taken your car to the service center that day. You might have been in the bathroom or out talking to the mechanic while that news segment aired, or Kelsey might have been on time. A series of Divine directional signals fell into alignment to make it possible for the requested tools to arrive. Everybody involved, from the boy and his family to Kelsey and the man who gave you the book, were part of this plan. On a soul level we are all connected this deeply, though on the earth plane we may appear to be strangers.

There are no coincidences, and timing is always perfect. If you'd read the story about Walter and Lancelot prior to hearing about the boy's death in the rock quarry, it would have been just an interesting story, and your soul would not have touched into it in the same way. So it was necessary to put the book aside for a few weeks, see the news report, and then pick up the book again to see the story about the two brothers in Scotland. This is how all human events are guided. This is how patterns of perfection work. Today was an exercise in these patterns for you.

As you know, every death transforms the people who are attached to that transitioning soul, and in this case, you and I have a connection to the soul of the boy for teaching purposes. He is part of your story because his death will have a profound impact on a new direction you take with your teaching.

You are thinking about how to help the guilt-filled brother. You think you can pray for his protection from guilt and suffering or for his comfort or peace. But you know that you can't protect him from that, because a struggle with guilt is part of his lesson plan. Certainly you can pray that someone will have comfort, but how will they access that comfort? How will it reach them? Will they be open to receiving it?

The only prayer that has any effect is a prayer that asks for an opening to higher guidance. In the story of Walter and Lancelot, the only way to comfort poor Walter was to give him a vision of his dead brother. In other words, to open a conduit to the Divine. Asking for that opening is the only intervention you can request for another person. The most powerful prayer for the grieving brother is one that asks that the guides and helpers will be allowed access to his consciousness so he can receive their support."

That summer at the hospice grief camp for children, I met a beautiful, melancholy girl about 13 years old. We worked together on some craft projects and also shared some time doing outdoor activities before she told me her story. She told me that her 5 year-old brother had died only three months earlier by hitting his head while playing in a rock quarry. Yes, it was the same boy, and in addition to the sister, the older brother was at camp that year too, though I never had the opportunity to meet him and I never knew until that day that there was a sister. I wondered if I should tell her the story of my seeing the news report at the car dealership, reading that chapter and receiving information from my guides, but I decided against it. In hospice work, we're trained to avoid discussing metaphysical topics with bereaved families (a policy that I don't fully support, as you'll see in Chapter 8). So instead, I held her and cried with her, saying a silent prayer that she would one day take a very deep breath and release her pain to Heaven, where guidance, comfort, joy and wisdom could be found.

5. Miracles, Messages and Manifestations: Recognizing Patterns of Perfection

Do you recall the story from Chapter 3 about the song "Scarlet Ribbons" and our expectations about the forms in which messages from Heaven should appear? In this chapter we'll look at the forms in which those messages actually *do* appear, and you may be surprised to find that you're already receiving them loud and clear.

HELLO AGAIN

One weekday afternoon last Spring I did something I rarely do. I flopped down on the couch to watch TV. This is uncharacteristic behavior because I'm generally a workaholic with two basic settings: "on" and "hyperdrive." My television watching is limited to Netflix movies and the yoga show every morning on FIT TV. For me to actually *sit down* and channel surf is as likely as the snowball's chance of survival in El Infierno.

But on this particular day I'd run out of inspiration and energy. I'd been working on a presentation about after-death communication for an upcoming seminar, but I was unfocused and edgy and couldn't concentrate. I'd been looking for a clever way to describe how we sabotage our ability to recognize Divine communication by clinging to fear-based religious superstitions, but couldn't think of any way to explain this adequately. I had no way of knowing at the time that the information I needed was on its way to me, courtesy of my local cable company.

I cruised through the pay per-view movie listings and a 1987 movie called *Hello Again* caught my eye because the summary said, "A suburban housewife dies and is brought back to life by her wacky sister." How could I resist?

In this movie, a woman (played by Shelley Long) dies. Her "wacky" sister owns a metaphysical bookstore and is portrayed as a stereotyped hippie mystic who wears flowing dresses and big earrings and says "oh wow" a lot while consulting the I Ching and Tarot. After Shelley dies, the wacky sister finds an old witchcraft book (only witches can talk to the dead, don't you know?) and brings Shelley back to life... in physical form. Shelley revisits the scene of her death (a hospital) where the handsome doctor (Gabriel Byrne) gives her blood tests to prove that she really is the woman who died in the ER several months earlier. Shelley, now fully acclimated to being undead, meddles in the lives of her husband and son to make everything better for them.

I didn't have a problem with most of it, but I was annoyed by the way interdimensional communication was characterized. The wacky hippie sister had to wear a cape with stars and moons on it, light candles in a graveyard, speak incantations in ancient languages and read from a dusty old book in order to communicate with her dead sister. And when spirits talk to her, they speak in a Vincent Price vampire voice... *"helllooooo, I am speeeaaaking to youuuu from the woooorrrlllld of the deeeaaaad."*

This is exactly why people don't believe they can hear from their loved ones on the Other Side. Because they're expecting Vincent Price and candles and suns and moons, and they don't realize that it's right there in front of them... without special effects!

There are two reasons why this story is important. It shows us how hackneyed and cliché our expectations of Divine communication are, but it also shows that the movie itself was a Divine communication to *me,* because when I "accidentally" stumbled upon that movie, I'd been looking for a teaching tool to explain this very thing. It happened the same way when I received the Scarlet Ribbons revelation; I'd been working on a presentation about prayer and manifestation, and wondering what to use as an example to explain how prayer works. Pop! Scarlet Ribbons shows up in my head. And when I'm wondering how to make an important statement about after-death communication, pop! This movie shows up.

We *all* get messages like this. They're beaming down upon us 24 hours a day. Every day. No exceptions. The trick is to open your mind and embrace the idea that they really are messages and not flukes of nature or coincidences. There *are* no coincidences.

Here are a few more interesting examples, some of which deliver a message with a gentle hand, and others that scare us to death in order to get our attention. Take a look:

Carly and the Kiosk

Last summer my dear friend Carly -- who'd been one of Danny's caregivers and loved him like her own child -- was visiting me from California. In the small town where I live, the locals rarely patronize the cute little gift shops downtown, but one day when Carly and I were driving through town returning home from a hike in the woods, she got a hankering to do some tourist-style shopping. Knowing that I needed to get home and didn't want to mosey through the shops with her, she suggested that I drop her off at the drug store and she'd browse around for a bit before walking the five blocks back to my house.

Normally I would have readily agreed, but for some reason I felt like going into the drug store with her. This is an expensive tourist-trap kind of store with a pharmacy, a gourmet kitchenware section and a counter that sells fancy imported chocolate. Not the kind of place I usually frequent. In fact, in the two years I'd lived in this town, I'd been into this store only once to fill an emergency prescription. But on this day I really wanted to go inside.

So there we were, hanging out in this store, and while Carly's looking at fancy candles and hand-blown wine glasses, I'm drawn to the CD kiosk where you can put on headphones and listen to music samples (another thing I never do... listen to music at a CD kiosk). There were 36 CDs to choose from, and I chose a collection of Celtic songs (without a list of song titles). I put on the headphones and from the automatic, randomly-selected lineup of songs comes *Danny Boy.*

Now, as you might imagine, this is a very important song to me, not just because of my own Danny, but because it's about the death of someone's son and the communication they have between dimensions.

I fall to pieces every time I hear it. But this time instead of dissolving into tears, I giggled, because I knew Danny sent it to me to say, "I'm here. Tell Carly hello from me." What was even more interesting is that none of the other songs in the kiosk started at the beginning of the song. They started at random points in the song because the system has them playing all the time, so when you select one, you never know where you're going to come in. I clicked into some of the other songs just to verify that this was true, and every time I went back to *Danny Boy*, it started at the beginning.

I have no doubt that Danny pulled me into that store just to give me that message, because it was so unusual for me to be in there. I could just as easily have dropped Carly off and gone home, which would have been much more typical of my behavior.

Sandy and the Snipers

This story is so bizarre and reaches so deeply into the process of changing someone's life that it's barely believable, but I swear it's true. It's so far-fetched that I hardly know how to tell it.

Sandy has been a close friend of mine for 25 years. During eight of those years she was married to an abusive, narcissistic man named Chuck. She tried to leave him several times, but didn't succeed until the universe sent her a message she couldn't ignore.

Sandy and Chuck lived in Malibu, California. Sandy worked nights and often drove home on Pacific Coast Highway at 2:00 in the morning. On this particular night she was driving north from Santa Monica and heard a loud, cracking sound a microsecond before the two back windows of her car shattered into smithereens. She was terrified, having a vague memory of news reports about a sniper in the area, so she drove straight to the police station. Sure enough, her windows had been shot out by a gun. She was too shaken up to drive home, so she called Chuck to tell him about the incident and ask him to come pick her up.

"Why did you wake me up for this? Don't you know I have an early meeting in the morning?" Chuck snarled. "The car still drives doesn't it? You can get home on your own. I need to go back to sleep."

This was typical of Chuck's responses. He was a nasty son-of-a-bitch.

She did try to drive home. And here's where the story gets really, really weird.

It's now close to 4 a.m. and Sandy is driving down the deserted highway once more. Suddenly in her headlights a man appears... with a gun pointed directly at her! A second later another man appears at the driver's side window. It's a carjacking! My brave friend Sandy, who's now hysterical from fear and fatigue, has the presence of mind to hit the gas and run down the guy with the gun. She drives like a maniac until she reaches the next police station along her route-- this one in Malibu.

The police take her report and go out to look for the carjackers. Sandy once again calls Chuck, because she's in no shape to drive the rest of the way home.

"What?!? You're waking me up again?" he bellowed. "Can't the cops drive you home?"

The cops drove her home and she divorced Chuck a few months later. She's now happily married to the most wonderful guy in the world.

The moral of the story is that if you don't heed the messages early when they're gentle and subtle, they'll get louder and more forceful until you do. Through the years of her marriage to Chuck, Sandy received countless signs, symbols and little miracles that tried to show her the truth of her situation. But like so many women married to men like Chuck, she ignored the signs and continued trying to make the marriage work. As time went by the signs got stronger, like the time Chuck "forgot" to show up for her 40th birthday party, or when, during one of her many short-lived separations from Chuck, she ran into an old flame who'd just gotten divorced and confessed that he still loved her after all these years. She had countless opportunities to change her life, but only snipers and carjackers could fully gain her attention.

These events were windows of opportunity, created as a joint venture between her soul and her guides to lead her toward some other options. The messages get louder and stronger until they are heeded, and for Sandy, it took the sniper/carjacking incident to convince her that it was time to leave Chuck.

None of the events in our lives are random or accidental. Sometimes we just have to learn our lessons the hard way. The more we become aware that our guides and angels are working with us and communicating with us, the more efficiently we can respond to their calls.

Molly's Special

This past winter I met a wonderful couple name Julie and Ron. Their daughter Molly had been killed in a car wreck eight months earlier, and they were deeply grieved. They had come to see me speak at a local church, and after the presentation they invited me to go to breakfast with them.

I asked one of the churchgoers to recommend a restaurant because I wasn't familiar with the neighborhood. He directed us to a small, popular local place, and while were looking over the menu, Julie's eyes filled with tears. The first item on the menu was called "Molly's Special." We all understood that Molly was letting us know that she not only approved of her parents making friends with me, but that she had a hand in orchestrating our meeting and was most certainly joining us for breakfast that day.

LITTLE SWAN FOR MOM

My mother has become very open to receiving psychic messages in recent years. She understands and accepts that I converse with Danny, and has received a few communications from him herself. After her husband Marty died, she began receiving subtle messages from him as well.

Each year on the anniversary of Marty's death, she comes to Oregon to spend a week with me so she doesn't have to be alone on his death anniversary, and we do a little ceremony to honor his passing. Last year when she was visiting, she was particularly sad and missing

Marty. One afternoon while she stayed home knitting and I took my daily walk in the woods, I asked Danny and my guides to do me a favor.

I said, "I never ask for magic tricks, but just for fun, will you send my mom a swan? Something to show her that Heaven is always close by and that she's not alone here on earth? Maybe let her see a swan on TV, or maybe we'll see one on the lake, or a picture of a swan in a magazine. Something, somewhere, anything, please." (The swan is an important animal totem for my entire family).

I planned to return from my walk and tell mom that I'd made this request, so that when a swan did show up (as I knew it would), she'd know it was the message I'd asked for. But as soon as I got home we got busy with some activity or another and I promptly forgot about the whole thing. It never entered my mind again... until the swan arrived.

Three days later when I went to walk in the woods again, I dropped mom off downtown because she likes to browse in the stores. When I picked her up an hour later, she was very excited to show me a little glass swan she'd purchased in an antique store. And that's when I remembered that I'd asked Danny to send her a swan. When I told her that I'd requested it for her, she was amazed but not surprised (she's used to this sort of thing by now). Sometimes it doesn't hurt to get a scarlet ribbon.

I could write ten books full of examples like this, but there's no need to, because you very likely have plenty of examples from your own life. All I can add to what you already know is this... trust that these experiences are not accidents or coincidences. They are very real communications from the many loving beings who walk with us at all times.

"We want you to know that we always hear singing, chanting, dreaming, crying, speaking, praying and any other form of calling out to Heaven. It is important for people to know this as they strive to increase their intuitive abilities. The first thing ones must know in order to do this is to believe without question that their thoughts, voices and prayers are not only heard, but become part of the movement of energy that fuels all the universe. This is why it's so important to keep the thoughts always on love and gratitude. Because these thoughts create the world. If you look at scriptural texts from all the world's major religions, you will understand that the word "creator" or "creation" is literal in the sense that everything is created from the thought forms of all the beings in the universe, whether embodied or not. Thought creates matter. It is *that* powerful."

INSULATION VS. VENTILATION

We don't necessarily need to be terrorized into listening to our own souls with dramatic scenarios like Sandy and her snipers, but at the same time it's also not always sweet and subtle like my mom and the swan. In fact, my mother once described it like this: "Our guides are always giving us clues and signposts, like a trail of pebbles to lead the way. It's up to us to pay attention to them. When we don't, the pebbles eventually become giant boulders dropped onto our heads. Sooner or later, we pay attention."

Messages from the higher realms come at us in hundreds of ways, loud and quiet, obvious and not-so-obvious, and like in Sandy's story, sometimes they're boulders dropped on our heads. Sometimes being blown open by shock is the only way anything can really reach us, because we are so *insulated* inside these dense physical bodies. Any time a hole is blown through that insulation it's a gift from the Divine, and those openings are often created by a traumatic experience like the death of a loved one or a profoundly powerful experience like falling in love.

The insulation keeps us locked into the ego realm and prevents Divine messages from coming through, and traumatic or powerful experiences rip the insulation/protective layer off of us. Once the insulation is pierced, we find ourselves walking around on earth saying, "How can I live with this open wound, this vulnerability where my heart is exposed? It's way too raw, way too dangerous." Certainly we can understand this feeling in someone whose world has been shattered by grief and loss, but even someone whose world has been brightened by romantic love experiences discomfort when the insulation is breached. So we instinctively re-insulate ourselves. Sometimes it's necessary in order to function in the world.

But at the same time it's important to find a balance where that opening can be alive and receptive, where we can invite the teachings in and experience gratitude for the opening. For me, that opening occurred through Danny's illness and death, and I have come to understand it as the greatest gift imaginable in all of life. And now my most sacred vow is to keep that opening alive and ventilated so that I can teach others how to do the same.

So how do we practice being ventilated rather than insulated? There is only one way that I know of, and that's through prayer and meditation.

Here on earth we spend most of our energy focused intently on the day-to-day drama of physical survival. We live at ground level; fearful and uncertain, scrambling for any little scrap of security to comfort and sustain us. We don't realize that only a few deep breaths away there are beautiful realms of higher energy available to us if we would only take a moment to stop and *connect*. Meditation is the tool that makes this connection possible. It shifts our focus and helps us become receptive to the vibrant energy streams that surround us, allowing us to tap into those streams for inspiration and information.

Meditation is about tapping *in* rather than tuning *out*. Contrary to popular belief, it's not necessarily about sitting up straight, emptying our minds and becoming blank. It's more about letting the body be as comfortable as possible so that relaxation can occur and the voice of our souls can be heard. In meditation the goal is to *listen*. Unlike traditional western prayer postures with bowed heads, closed eyes, clasped hands and constricted bodies, in meditation we open our bodies and our hearts, with our faces lifted to the light. Our bodies, with our breath as a conduit, become powerful receivers, inviting healing energy to flow through us.

Meditation is not the same as prayer, but it works hand-in-hand with prayer. A prayer is a request broadcast to the universe. It is *output*. Meditation is the process of receiving the answer to that prayer. It is *input*. While this may seem like a simple formula, it comes with an enormous challenge... getting our egos out of the way. Instead of praying for the things that give us a sense of security on earth (health, money, relationships), the only prayer that truly connects us is a prayer that says "lead me to the highest good in this situation."

The next step is to be quiet and listen. A regular practice of meditation -- especially if you keep a meditation journal -- will open up a new world of peace and possibility. And every prayer that asks only to reveal the truth and the highest good will always be answered.

I SURRENDERED TO GOD AND LOST MY JOB

Why should we communicate with the higher realms? Why meditate? Why be spiritual at all?

Because the more open we are to Divine guidance -- which comes from a clear, clean place, free of our ego's agenda -- the more sense our lives will make. Because there is so much more going on than just what we perceive with our five physical senses. Because emotional pain can be paralyzing, and accessing levels of consciousness beyond the emotional or the psychological can free us from that pain.

But it's a big commitment. Once you open up to these levels you can't return to insulation and the limited life of the ego. Once you start really focusing on manifestation, your world will fall apart in order to be rebuilt anew, and the more you receive that with gratitude, the faster the changes will happen until ultimately, you'll learn how to flow with those change and not resist so much. The real gift is not that you manifest a new job or a big house or a happy marriage. The real gift is that you learn to listen to your soul and to trust its wisdom. Without this type of complete trust and surrender, you are living by default, moving forward robotically, and you're in pain because you're trying to control everything, resisting everything. If you lose your job, you grieve, you worry, you have fear, and that's OK. The guides would never tell you to judge yourself for being fearful, but they *would* tell you to be with the fear, to breathe into it, allow it, process it, learn from it, feel it, and then walk through it to the new reality that awaits you.

How often should you stop and surrender? Whenever you feel the pain of resistance. Just stop and move through it. Visualize yourself as a non-physical spirit, a ghost, and imagine you are simply, calmly, walking through a wall. Do this a hundred times a day if you need to. It will lift you to a higher consciousness and bring you into the present.

How do you surrender?

You stop *projecting.* Stop broadcasting fear. Stop *everything.* Stop trying to survive. Stop working so hard. Just STOP. And then broadcast one sentence, one word, one thought of surrender, and it will shift everything. Don't ask to be rescued. Don't ask God to fix it for you. Ask only to see the truth and lesson in the situation. And, here's the real trick... you say it with *gratitude,* with love. Not with fear, cynicism or anger. You say, "I surrender with love. I surrender with trust. I put myself into the arms of the angels and I will STOP and just BE exactly where I am."

There is an Arabic word -- Inshallah-- that a great teacher once taught me to use as an expression of surrender.[15] It literally translates into "The will of Allah be done," or "God's will be done." When I lived in a tiny, isolated cabin at the edge of a deep canyon gorge and was struggling with the most intense fear and emotional devastation of my life, I would sometimes stand at the canyon's edge and scream this word to the sky and the river below. One day after doing this, I returned to the cabin, checked my email and phone messages (do you think I'd live in a cabin without a high speed internet connection?) only to learn that I'd just been laid off from a lucrative freelance job that I'd had for the past *seven years.*

Sometimes surrender can produce instant results. I'd had reservations about that job all along, because my employer was corrupt and unscrupulous and I never really felt comfortable working for him even though I stayed in his employ for seven years. I was poised on the brink of change. I'd asked the universe to move me toward my soul's chosen work as an author and teacher, and in order for that shift to occur, things had to move around and open up a space for change. It's a slow, painful process, but it's in this process that our souls expand. Anybody who cares about consciousness would never choose to avoid these experiences.

---

[15] http://en.wikipedia.org/wiki/Insha%27Allah

Taking this example a step further, the loss of that job threw me into a ghastly financial crisis just as I was preparing to move into a house I'd just purchased. The monthly payments were huge, and without this job there was no way I could make ends meet. I managed for the first year by taking in roommates and doing as many small freelance jobs as I could scare up, but a year later the economy collapsed and the freelance work disappeared. Like millions of Americans at the beginning of 2009, I couldn't find work and my house was headed for foreclosure.

But it turned out to be a gift. During the year-long foreclosure process I was able to live in my house without making any mortgage payments. I'd bought the house with no money down, and because of the sunken real estate market it had no equity, so I really wasn't losing any money. Yes, my credit was ruined, but I was able to live rent-free for a year, which gave me time to write this book and focus on developing my workshops and related endeavors. It was a miracle! I'd prayed for help with my financial problems, and the universe basically said, "Sure, how about living rent-free for a year? Would that help?"

And bingo! It was just what I needed. Most people would find this situation intolerable, but I was able to follow the unfolding of events with an open heart, and allow this seemingly tragic circumstance to lead me to a new life. Not only did it give me time to write a book and create a new career strategy, but letting go of my house freed me to move to another city where I could go to school to finish a degree in religious studies. That degree is something I'm certain my guides wanted me to pursue because of the credibility it would add to my work. I felt like I was being moved along like a slot car on a track. Inshallah indeed!

I was once interviewed on a radio show and the host said, "If you understand these processes so well, then your life must be really peaceful and balanced. It seems that your life would be really perfect."

I laughed out loud and choked on the water I was sipping.

I explained to him that what the ego wants and what the soul wants are usually in opposition to each other. My ego, given free reign, would create a life of comfort and ease, but my soul prefers a life of growth and experience. I told him-- and the radio audience --

that my house was in foreclosure and I couldn't afford health insurance. I also revealed that I'd left a demoralizing marriage three years ago am still too traumatized to open my heart to someone again. In other words, I have the same human struggles that everyone else has, but I recognize and accept those struggles as the work required for my soul's growth. So in that sense, yes, my life *is* perfect. Once we begin to embrace conflict and uncertainty, we can deal with death, divorce, illness, poverty and all kinds of troublesome experiences from a higher perspective. We begin to learn, through these experiences, how to ventilate, how to walk through walls, how to release resistance and BE with the experience.

THAT is the secret.

6. The Inter-Dimensional Superhighway

"The true meaning of sin is to be separate from Divine energy. The true meaning of faith is to live your life with the knowledge that Divine energy is always available to us, always guiding, helping and loving us. Asking for its guidance and receiving it occur simultaneously."

Danny

"Ask, and it shall be given you; seek, and ye shall find; knock, and it shall be opened unto you: For every one that asketh receiveth; and he that seeketh findeth; and to him that knocketh it shall be opened."

The Bible, Matthew 7:7

Many of you will remember the term "information superhighway," which was used during the early 1990s to describe the internet and the vast amount of data whizzing through it. There's a metaphysical equivalent of this system that we like to call the *interdimensional* superhighway, which describes the conduit through which we receive Divine guidance.

The internet is an exquisite analogy for interdimensional communication. I mentioned earlier how tuning in to the higher realms is similar to changing channels on a tv or radio, and how these realms are broadcasting to us at all times. These messages are sent to us in ways that can be compared to sending an email. It is hard to comprehend this because we're so locked into to a linear understanding of the physical world that it's we can't believe telepathic communication is as viable as physical communication. We think that "imagining" conversation with a "dead" person isn't as good as having their physical presence, because we don't have the comprehension of how much communication is occurring energetically, on levels that can't be experienced with the five senses.

David Staume in *The Athiest Afterlife* gives an excellent example to explain the existence of other dimensions. I'm paraphrasing here and adding a bit of my own spin to it, but basically he asks us to imagine that we're in a train speeding through the countryside and we're looking out the window. The scenery is constantly changing, but if we're inside looking straight out the window we only perceive one scene at a time... the scene that's framed by the window. The previous scenes and the scenes yet to come are not in our awareness, so it appears that they don't exist. But if we open the window and stick our heads out, we can turn to the left and the right and see a section of the previous and upcoming scenes at the same time we're experiencing the present scene. And as we're observing them, these scenes are shifting in small ways according to our distance from them, the angle from which they're viewed and other factors. We can also look up toward the sky or down toward the ground. We've now added new dimensions to our perception. Instead of looking out the window from inside the train to one particular view or dimension, we've added several dimensions by moving outside the window and looking around us.

Once we understand that these extra dimensions are available to us, we can begin learning how to work with them. The internet, as a rough model of telepathic communication, is actually training us to understand the speed and power of thought. This shift to higher understanding is obvious when you look at our rapid advances in technology. There is an estimated 2.7 billion questions asked of Google every month.[16] How did we find answers to those questions before we had Google? We went to libraries and read books, or we asked each other, and we transferred information on a very slow, analog level. But now most of the information in the world is literally at our fingertips, and it's moving among us faster and faster every day. The universe is expanding right before our eyes, and it's all being directed by Heaven. Now that we've created the technical tools for transmitting all this effectively, we are getting closer to grasping the concept of a universe that's always broadcasting information.That's a big step toward achieving interdimensional communication.

---

[16] http://www.youtube.com/watch?v=pMcfrLYDm2U&feature=related (A video by Karl Fisch and Scott McLeod)

Many people ask me to explain how communication with my guides travels through dimensions and why some people receive it and others don't.

Communication from the higher realms (which we call Heaven) is always present, always "on" and always broadcasting. These communications can be received by anyone who seeks them when the mind is open, calm and clear, and we will always receive the exact information we need at any given time. It's like tuning on the TV and selecting a program to watch, but the signal has to be clear, and there are many elements that can obstruct it. People who understand telepathy and channeling know how certain emotions such as anger, blame and a belief in powerlessness, can inhibit these communications. This is because those feelings instill a belief in separateness; a sense that we are not connected to the teachers, the Source, the mother, father God itself. When we live with a belief in this type of un-connectedness, we cannot channel.

Many people ask me, "why do people who've never been psychic suddenly hear from loved ones who have died?" And the answer is that grief opens the heart, especially if the grief is processed with spiritual awareness. If you feel that a loved one was "taken" unfairly and you harbor anger and blame toward God, the world at large or a particular individual, you would be less likely to receive such a communication because the lines are clogged up by these feelings. But there are always exceptions, because sometimes communication can come through to help redirect you toward a higher way of thinking. Depending on your state of mind, such a communication may or may not be heeded (remember Sandy and the snipers?)

These communications often come in symbolic forms, not through literally hearing or seeing, but through dreams, visions and so-called "coincidences." It is never a coincidence that a certain book comes into your possession at a certain time, or you run into a long lost friend "accidentally." The story of my friend whose late father was a decorated WW2 fighter pilot illustrates this perfectly.

She was walking in the park thinking of him on his birthday the year after he died, and looked into the sky just in time to see a vintage airplane fly over and tip its wings! She couldn't figure out what that plane was doing there until she later learned that there had been an air show in a neighboring town that day. She thought it was a remarkable coincidence until she realized that she just happened to be outside walking at that particular time, and happened to look up in the sky. She could have been at home doing her laundry or in the grocery store when that plane flew over, but instead she was out walking with a clear view of the sky above her. It most certainly was not a coincidence, but a clear message from her father. All of these are the forms in which spirit communicates with us. For people who want to tune in to transmissions from loved ones, guides, angels, God and the higher self, it is first necessary to practice recognizing these alleged coincidences as actual messages.

Messages from Heaven have to travel through many filters in order to reach us, and these filters are dense and resistant in most people. This is why meditation and visualization is such an important tool for *allowing* Heaven. We've talked about ventilation and opening the mesh and the layers of density. Another way to see it is to imagine the filters getting finer and finer until they are no longer visible, like a fabric becoming more and more threadbare until it simply thins out and disappears.

When you begin to channel and receive, you will often feel as if you're just making it up. This is because   the limitations of the mind, such as logic, linear time and three physical dimensions, can be difficult to break through. Transmissions from the higher realms have to be translated into a form we can understand in human language and symbols, and this is a foreign language compared to the pure frequency of energy from which these messages originate. The translation process is a big undertaking, and requires your human intellect to translate them into your own, familiar brain waves, thought patterns and words. This is why it often feels like the words you're receiving are your own and the symbols and messages are simply products of your imagination.

But with practice, the energy that accompanies these messages will start to feel different than your normal energy. You might feel a sensation in your body, a tingling or excitement in your chest, or perhaps a deep relaxation and subtle feeling of being dazed or spaced out, which signals that you are opening to receive. Different people feel this in different ways, and some people who are very experienced in channeling don't feel any bodily sensations at all, because the process has become so natural and integrated for them.

As you begin to get more confident that the impression you're receiving are real, you'll become aware of a sense of timelessness, and you'll notice that the gap between requesting contact and receiving it doesn't exist at all. The energetic signals are sent and received at the speed of thought, so conversations between dimensions happen instantly, with no lag time. Because information from Heaven is being broadcast all the time, we don't have to wait for somebody on the other end to come up with an answer to our questions. The information is already out there just waiting to be picked up.

It's similar to the way in which a digital fax machine works. You dial a number to send an image of the page. The image is recorded and stored digitally, and a few moments later it is sent to the recipient. Because there is no linear time in the higher realms, the messages can be created, stored, sent and received all at the same time without piling up into a giant interdimensional logjam. It's like a living library of information that we can access whenever we choose, the same way we choose to watch television. The signals are being sent all the time, but you only receive them when you turn on the tv. You can turn it on and off a thousand times a day if you want to, so that you'll receive exactly the information you ask for whenever you ask for it. The information your soul chooses to receive will gently filter down into your awareness. Remember, it's not linear… this dimension doesn't exist in a straight line, so the messages aren't lined up like airplanes on a taxiway waiting for clearance. They exist everywhere at once.

When I first started channeling there seemed to be a time gap between the asking and the receiving of information, because I was working so hard to make it happen. I'd create a quiet meditation space, maybe light a candle, set up my little voice recorder and concentrate on receiving. While I did get messages this way, I quickly learned that for me, this type of concentration was serious overkill. I discovered that the more relaxed and casual I was about it, the easier it was to open a dialog. As a writer by nature and by profession, I eventually figured out that if I wanted to converse with my guides, I could do it by simply sitting at my computer and typing whatever impressions came to me. I also realized that when I was teaching a class or a workshop, all I had to do was a quick check-in with my guides to ask for their assistance, and the words and ideas would start flowing through me with ease. In fact, it isn't possible for me to teach without them. It isn't possible for me to do anything without them. And this is true for you, too.

About two years into my interdimensional relationship with Danny and my other guides, I noticed an energetic shift. The sense of separation had disappeared completely and I could no longer tell the difference between my words and theirs. It was as if they had merged with me so fully that everything I expressed when I was teaching or writing was a composite of their energy and mine. A few years earlier a psychic told me that my relationship with my friends in the higher realms was like being in an airplane and looking down at a swimming pool on the ground below, but with practice -- and above all, faith -- it would soon be as if I was *in* the swimming pool. I sensed that the time had come for this to happen, and I asked my guides about it:

"Once you've crossed into the 'swimming pool' of Divine love, your thoughts and our thoughts will occur at the same moment, because we are communicating on a plane of consciousness where we're both *creating* at the same time. You will find that typing isn't fast enough for recording the transmissions we send, because they will occur simultaneously with your asking for them. We will speak *through* you, and as you write and teach, we will be helping you verbalize our messages. We send you impressions made of light, color, sound and energy, and your body converts them into human thought forms and language. Your body, mind, brain, perspective, language and experience are required in order for this type of translation to happen.

It is important for you to teach others that the guides *want* to make contact. They are ecstatic when they're able to make a connection with someone on earth, especially if that person is sharing the information with others. The guides are teaching souls, and communicating is what they do best. When they find an open conduit, they jump through it with glee and gratitude. Here is an analogy that will help you understand how the guides respond to people on earth. Imagine the higher beings are above the earth looking down at it (not that there's really an up or down in a linear, directional sense) and what they see is something like a thick sea of fog. In this fog (or the veil, as seen from Heaven) are little openings, little holes in the fog where light comes through and reaches the guides. These holes are the psychic conduits of people who are open to receiving. They are like beacons that call out to Heaven, and the guides are eager to find these openings and begin a dialog."

This view through the fog is beautifully illustrated in a story told by Carolyn Weislogel,[17] a lovely, gifted woman who works with angels and told the following story at a workshop I attended in 2006.

Carolyn was driving on Interstate 77 in Parkersburg, West Virginia. She could see flashing lights up ahead, an ambulance and a fire truck, and realized that there had been a serious accident. When she got closer to the scene she saw a dead body lying on the grass covered with a tarp, and a moment later she sensed a presence next to her that seemed to be electrified with excitement. She heard the presence exclaim, "Hey lady! I'm still alive! I'm not dead! Wow! I had no idea it would be like this! All that happened was I got freed from that hard physical body, and I'm still here! I'm still alive! Please lady, you have to tell my family that I'm still alive!"

Carolyn was used to conversing with angels, but this was the first time a newly-dead person had contacted her. Apparently upon leaving his body, he'd been delighted to discover that he had not gone into oblivion, and was eager to share the news with his family. Hundreds of people had driven past his body, but Carolyn was the only one with an open conduit. The dead man saw her light shining through the fog.

"I'm sorry," Carolyn said, "but I don't think I can help you. I don't know who your family is."

---

[17] http://www.angelharps.com

The man said, "You'll find them. Please tell them that my time on earth was complete, and if this accident had not taken my life, there was something else in the works that would have. Please tell them how clearly I understand this, and that I want them to understand it too, but mostly I want them to know that I still exist."

Carolyn realized that news of the accident was likely to appear in the Parkersburg newspaper the next day, so she looked it up online and the story was there, giving the man's name. She watched the paper for the next few days until his obituary appeared, giving his wife's name and address, and she knew that despite her fear of potentially causing more pain for the wife, she had to tell the grieving woman about the message her husband wanted to send. Carolyn gathered up her nerve and made the call, prefacing her news with condolences and an assurance that the wife was in her prayers. Then she told the story, not knowing what kind of response to expect. To Carolyn's surprise the wife was completely open, and through grateful tears thanked Carolyn again and again for helping to ease her pain.

"Imagine that all the solar systems and all the bodies and objects in the universe are a connect-the-dots game, and there are lines drawn from one object to another to connect them. This is a physical representation of the interdimensional superhighway. This may help you understand how everything in the universe -- animal, mineral, plants, other life forms, all the elements and everything seen and unseen -- is pulsing and breathing together as part of one living body of energy. These lines of connection are like the jumble of electric cords behind your desk that connect you to the world via your computer system. The information being sent through the holes in the fog is sent through these lines, just like the information from the internet is sent through the cords that connect your monitor, computer, modem and phone or cable line.

Just as we can send messages to you, your thoughts, prayers and intentions are broadcast back to us through those same lines, though of course I'm only speaking symbolically, since there's no literal "back and forth." Everyone and everything is plugged into this grid, and people on earth are accessing this information all the time, whether or not they're aware of it."

CAN EVERYBODY RECEIVE THESE MESSAGES?

Yes. Absolutely. No question about it. Everyone *can* and everyone *does*.

Millions of people across religions, nations and cultures have interdimensional experiences, whether in the form of visitations from the dead, premonitions, near-death experiences, out-of-body experiences, sensing of energy, lucid dreaming, healing ability and hundreds of variations on these forms. All this information comes from the same source, the vibrational realm that I refer to as "Heaven," which has nothing to do with the Heaven you learned about as a child where angels float around in the clouds and there are pearly gates and golden thrones. Though depending on one's perspective, one could certainly experience it that way.

In Don Piper's book about his near-death experience, *90 Minutes in Heaven*, he describes Heaven exactly that way, with an angelic choir, pearly gates and all the biblical trimmings. Don's Heaven only included Christians however, and much of his book is focused on his belief that non-Christians will experience the fire, darkness and torment of hell when they die (though he concedes on his website that there may be a special provision for Jews, because without them Christianity would not be possible).

In my reality, there is no sense of separateness in the higher realms. But I also know that everybody is on their own path to awareness, and we will each experience whatever we need in our journey toward Love and Oneness. Those who believe that only a select few have the privilege of a direct relationship with God and Heaven will receive loving healing and guidance on the Other Side to gently move them toward a more inclusive view.

Earlier this year I attended a "Christian hands-on healing demonstration" at the local coffee hangout in my town. The energy in the room was lovely when I arrived; everybody was singing hymns and hugging and praising God, and it was very inviting and inspiring. I'd never been in a gathering like this before and was very interested, especially when members of the group took turns standing up and saying, "I received a word of knowledge from God" about this or that.

Many of the people in the room received these words of knowledge, and some of them pinpointed specific issues in other people that needed healing, such as "I received a word of knowledge from God that somebody in this room has pancreatic cancer." And sure enough, someone with pancreatic cancer would come forward to be healed. Eventually the whole event turned into a sea of hugging, praying, crying people laying hands on each other and calling for healing from God. They even used words like "supernatural" to describe the power that was working through them.

I was amazed. I could feel the healing energy in the room, and could see that these folks were tapping into to something sacred and powerful. At one point a woman came up to me and said, "God just told me that you are grieving over the death of a loved one." She was right, of course, and I agreed to let her put her hand on my heart and pray for me to find peace. Did I mention that I was amazed? These people were *channeling!*

I was so impressed that I called the leader of this group the next day to interview him for this book. I loved the idea of getting a Christian perspective on channeling, because in my perception, this man and his followers understood that we're all getting our direction from the same Source. He was happy to hear from me when I told him how moved I was by the gathering. But the conversation quickly disintegrated when I told him, with great love and exuberance, how much I could sense the Oneness present in that room. They were doing the same thing all healers do when they tune into God for guidance. The same thing that I do as a channeler; working with Divine energy to create love and healing.

The C word -- channeler -- fell with a thud into the middle of the conversation. He emphatically stated, "This is *not* channeling. We work with the Holy Spirit, and that's directly from God. Channeling is The Devil trying to imitate the miracles of God. It's not Divine energy. We have the Holy Spirit talking to us through the name of Jesus Christ, and that's the only way healing is possible."

When I replied, still lost in my naïve exuberance, "Yes, I understand. Isn't it beautiful the way God connects with us? Whether you call it the Holy Spirit, Divine energy, channeling, words of knowledge, the Great Spirit, it's all the same thing, it's all universal love, isn't it?"

He said, "No. It's not the same thing. The only way to work with the Holy Spirit is to accept Jesus Christ as your savior, and the only people who can receive this kind of guidance are those who come to Christ."

He went on to tell me that anybody who does not connect to God through Jesus (his version of Jesus) does not have a "complete connection" and will not be allowed into Heaven. I asked him if this would be true for a Buddhist monk who spent his entire life in meditation and prayer, helping the sick, serving the community and thinking about nothing *but* God. His answer was, "That's a false God."

Ouch!

As someone who was not raised with biblical fundamentalism, I was surprised to discover how protected I'd been from what many people experienced when they questioned their childhood religions. They felt rejected and invalidated because their intuitive impressions didn't jive with the religious requirements of their families and cultures, and were told that they'd be forbidden entrance to Heaven.

This hit me like a punch in the stomach, and it *hurt*. Now I understand how people feel when they are told that Divine love is only available to them if they meet certain conditions. This man was telling me that my experience of the Divine, which has been beautiful, healing and beneficial to myself and others, is not adequate, and the Divine experiences of Buddhists in Tibet, Aborigines in Australia and Pygmies in the Congo are not only false, but are the product of an evil force.

How does one respond to something like this?

With love, of course. It's a great opportunity to practice compassion and the release of judgment. I never talked to that preacher again, and I'm still working to release my judgments about him and his congregation while mourning the loss of their potential for spreading love and healing. But I needed to tell that story because it says so much about separation vs. oneness. It is never, ever about pitting one group of people against another, or reserving Heaven for a chosen group. That is not Love. And God *is* love.

97

One day when I was struggling with sadness and hopelessness, I had a revelation about asking for help. I can't remember why I was so sad that day, but I knew I could find peace by checking in with my guides. But I was too stressed and caught up in the drama of my predicament to relax and surrender to higher guidance.

I tried every meditation technique I knew, but nothing worked. I toyed with the idea of logging on to one of my favorite websites (www.OrinDaben.com) to use one of the excellent guided meditations they offer, but found myself saying, "No! That would be cheating! I can do this myself! I don't need a guided meditation. I'm the person who teaches *other* people how to meditate! I don't need any help."

I instantly recognized the folly of this thinking and had to concede that my ego was *really* in the way.

So I went to the website looking for a meditation for releasing dark energies and blockages. As soon as I heard the beautiful, soothing voice of Sanaya Roman, the channeler who leads the meditations with the help of her guide Orin, I started to cry. I could instantly feel myself falling into the depths of Divine Love (the true meaning of *falling in love*), and could feel Danny and all my precious teachers around me. As I followed Sanaya's instructions and let myself be led into the meditation, I discovered something incredible.

It's not a cliché to say that we're never alone in the universe. If indeed we are all made from the same light, then one person's struggle is everybody's struggle. When one person -- one piece of the collective -- calls out to Spirit, it energizes the flow from the Source to the collective. So asking for help -- via prayer, meditation, channeling or whatever method you use -- is never about asking an "outsider" to step in and intervene, because there *are* no outsiders. When we ask a guide to help us, we're simply asking one part of the collective to assist another part. It's like washing your hands; both hands are part of the same body, and one hand assists the other, the same way the brain assists the legs to walk or the mouth to form words. We're all one body, and every part is connected to every other part. Communing with beings in the spirit world is one of the tools we're given on earth.

This ability to reach through the fog to the higher realms is a built-in support mechanism. When one part of the organism falters, we simply take energy from another part. That's what asking for help is all about.

In my distressed situation that day, I realized that I couldn't get unstuck on my own, so I reached out for OrinDaben, and got the boost I needed. And in the process I learned that it's OK to ask for help when I'm not capable of doing the work myself. For someone as headstrong and independent as I am, this was a major news flash.

Most people know intellectually that it's OK to ask for help, but they struggle with pride and a fear of losing their self-reliance. If we aren't even comfortable asking our best friends for help, it makes a whole lot of sense to ask our invisible friends instead.

"Our relationships with beings in other realms are partnerships, in the same way our relationship with Source is a partnership. There are several intersting parallels between interdimensional communication and human communication. In a healthy human relationship, you don't sit there and wait for the other person to do all the reaching and all the communicating. You have to meet in the middle. Each person has to take a step forward, and sometimes this requires a huge leap of faith. You have to believe that the other person *wants* to communicate with you. You have to trust that what they're saying is the truth, and you have to accept what you hear, even if you don't like it. In human relationships, communication shuts down when trust shuts down, and it is the same way with interdimensional conversation.

You have to reach out to us, and we have to reach out to you. There's an enormous amount of trust involved, particularly on your part, because you don't have the same level of knowledge and faith that we have. For us it's a matter of KNOWING that we can do this. For you, because of the armor of ego, it's requires BELIEVING. Every attempt at connection exercises your believing muscle.

Interdimensional communication uses a lot of energy, and many people, especially when they're new to it, find it mentally and physically exhausting. You have to train yourself to work in the higher frequencies, the same way a marathon runner trains for higher and higher levels of exertion and strength. This is why communication doesn't occur as easily when strong emotion is present. Sadness, anger, fear and doubt will drain your energy, and there's not much left over for transmission. If you would like to train that muscle, begin by spending ten minutes every day sitting in a quiet place with pen and paper, breathing deeply and making this request of your guides: *I open myself to your guidance today. Surround me with light and lead me to wisdom and truth in everything I do."* Then write down whatever comes through. If you do this every day, you will begin to receive guidance. This is the power of prayer. We are with you all the time, always supporting you."

A WORD ABOUT "NEGATIVE ENTITIES"

Many New Age practitioners believe that when we channel or meditate we should be careful about allowing negative entities or dark energies into our consciousness. According to what my guides tell me (and my own personal experience), this almost never happens. The only way a negative entity can attach itself to us or come into our energy field is if something very strong in our own reality is calling for our attention. But there are many authors, teachers and counselors out there who scare their audiences with admonishments like, "be careful if you try to do intuitive work or channeling, because you might attract negative energies."

While it is certainly possible to have a frightening experience while traveling through the higher realms, those experiences rarely, if ever, come from outside forces. In the words of my friend Marietta Roby, "there are no negative entities; only negative life experiences (past and current) which need to be acknowledged and understood so they can be healed."

Just this morning I did a Tarot reading for a woman who said, "I tried to meditate once but a negative entity came in and scared me so much I never tried it again."

This is heartbreaking! She gave up a world of beautiful spiritual connection because of fear. I told her that the sensation or presence she felt was an aspect of her Self that is needing love and healing. And it turns out, as we did the Tarot reading, that she had a lot of repressed experience and emotion that has never been brought into the light and processed.

So please don't be afraid. If you have a frightening experience in meditation or channeling, simply state, out loud, "I would like to understand and work with this energy to move it toward the Light." And it will shift immediately.

DREAMS

Daily meditation is an excellent way to get things flowing through the conduit. And once you get into the habit of writing down the messages that come through in meditation, you might also want to start recording your dreams in a dream journal.

The dream landscape is one of the most powerful guidance systems we have, because in dreams we are working in the higher planes of consciousness and receiving symbols and imagery directly from our souls. My dream life is so active that it interrupts my sleep; I'm usually woken up every hour or two by intense dreams. Though it would be nice to sleep through the night once in a while, I would never trade my dream guidance for a good night's sleep. I keep a digital voice recorder on my bedside table, and if the dream feels important enough, I record it for later transcription into my dream journal. I've been keeping a dream journal since 1998, and it is an outstanding record of my soul's work. If you have trouble remembering your dreams, daily meditation and journaling will help.

Dreams are absolutely spiritual, but they also contain a psychological aspect, because our spiritual curriculum is acted out through our behavior. Psychology, metaphysics and mythology meet up and dance beautifully together in our dreamscapes. As an example of spiritual dream interpretation, I'm going to share two remarkable dreams that illustrate how our guides work with us in the dream world. The first dream was astutely interpreted for me by my friend Rebecca Covington, who is a gifted channeler and uses that skill to decipher dreams.[18] The second dream was explained to me by Danny himself, via an interdimensional conversation we had the next day:

Dream # 1:

I was in a house with my ex-husband Jack, and the phone rang. It was a woman calling to tell me that she had three babies for me to adopt because their parents had been killed. The next thing I knew the three babies were in the house. The babies all had dirty diapers. I changed and cleaned them and Jack helped me.

The first baby was about four months old, extraordinarily beautiful and very large. And it could talk! It told me something wonderful and brilliant about why these babies came to me, but I can't remember what it said. The second baby was a girl, just a normal baby, and the third one was tiny, the size of a child's shoe. I didn't see it at first because it was hidden under some blankets.

While cleaning up the babies I remembered that I still had some of Danny's special medicated soap in the bathroom. I tore the bathroom apart looking for it. I really wanted to adopt the babies but couldn't imagine how to take care of them at my age, and I asked the woman if her agency was aware of how old I am. I hoped the state would give me some money for them. I also didn't want to raise them with Jack.

Rebecca's comments:

Of course the bigger, male baby said something brilliant because that was Danny! And the female baby, the "normal" one, was *you*, in the middle, between the very evolved Danny (the large baby who could speak) and the tiny baby hidden under the blankets (an aspect of you which has not emerged yet). Danny is acting as a guide, and the baby in the middle is you *now*, while the tiny, hidden baby is who you are becoming. That hidden baby is still weak and represents the emergence of something that has been restricted but is now being allowed to develop.

When you were cleaning the babies you wanted to wash them using some old "stuff," but you couldn't find it, because the old stuff (habits, belief

---

[18] www.RebeccaCovington.com

systems, old energies) doesn't work any more. The cleaning is about creating a new way of functioning that is no longer under the dark energy of your marriage to Jack. The death of the babies' parents represents this old energy, which has died off so that these new aspects of your self and your work can grow up clean and new.

This next dream came to me at a time when I was doubting my ability to channel and wondering whether I was truly qualified to teach and write about Divine guidance. I was still in the process of releasing some of the emotional fibers that held me to my ex husband, so there was enormous cleansing and shifting going on. Dreams like this are affirmations that we are on the right track and that our guides are walking beside us. They're always paying attention, and always communicating with us.

Sometimes dreams are cryptic and symbolic like the dream about the babies, and at other times they can be so clear that they're almost literal. On Mother's Day 2009 I had the following dream, and the next day I had a remarkable channeled conversation with Danny about it.

Dream # 2:

I was in a house cleaning the refrigerator, and suddenly realized that I didn't know where Danny was. Was he at school? Who was babysitting with him? He should have been home. How could I have forgotten him?

I went to his bedroom and there he was, waking up from a nap. He was smiling and happy and seemed to be about 7 or 8 years old, but he was wearing a diaper, and he'd had a bowel movement during his nap. I said, "I'm so sorry I forgot about you, I'm so sorry about the poop, I'll clean it up, I'm sorry! I'm so happy to see you!" He was giggling and we were hugging and laughing, delighted to be together. I started to clean him up *[notice the poop cleaning theme in both dreams?]*, and he said, "Don't worry, it doesn't bother me at all, I'm happy to see you too!" He jumped happily out of bed, and we laughed and played.

Then we went into the back yard and were met by a man who was our neighbor... the house was a side-by-side duplex and he lived in the other unit *[the Other Side!]*. He was an artist, and he showed me a catalog he was designing that advertised businesses related to spiritual teaching and healing. He opened it to a page that had an ad for my business of teaching people how to talk to Heaven. In the ad was an illustration of a woman in the sky -- a grieving mother -- looking down, with tears falling toward the earth. On the earth was an oak tree with its roots spreading deep into the ground. I knew there was something under the tree but I couldn't see it, but then he revealed it to me. It was a little spirit child below the earth.

I knew this dream was a Mother's Day gift from Danny, and I knew he sent it because he had an important message for me. The next day we had this conversation:

ME: Thank you for that dream! I used to hate Mothers Day, but now you've made it sacred for me. You've given me such amazing gifts.

DANNY: The gift I give you is the birth of your true Self. You have been so devoted and honest in this work, and you will introduce a healing Mother/Goddess energy to the grieving mothers you'll be working with in the future. I gave you that dream so you could include it in the book, and you will find the right spot for it. We are guiding you in this. We are delighted to have you with us, to work with you between worlds, and we are honored to be your servants in this work!

ME: How, do you work with my dreams? How does that happen?

DANNY: According to the pre-birth agreements we made to do this teaching together, you've given me a backstage pass to your soul, and there's a lot going on behind the scenes. I can plug into your soul's activity because we agreed to give each other access on this level. When I appear in your dreams, I'm supervising your subconscious processes, and I'm helping with whatever process the dream represents. Your other guides are involved as well. We send you dreams to illustrate movement in your consciousness, to help you look at various aspects of your Self. There is a reason why I appear at different ages and in different physical states, such as a baby, or a seven-year old, or in a wheelchair vs. able-bodied. It is because I -- in agreement with your soul -- am working to keep connected to the energy of *mothering*. It is important for you not to lose sight of this. It opens a certain place in your heart; an opening that is necessary in order to help other bereaved parents.

ME: I don't know how to thank you. I want to just disappear into Heaven with you.

DANNY: You are *already* in Heaven with us! Trust this beyond doubt. In the dream I showed you that our interdimensional relationship is as solid as an oak tree. I also showed you that I am happy in Heaven and have no suffering at all. No trauma or injury from the "poop" that you carry with you as a result of the senseless guilt you feel over my death. All bereaved parents feel this guilt, and cleaning it up it is an important part of the healing process. I am completely clean, and you can be too.

ME: Sometimes I feel that if I give up my guilt, I will be "cheating on" my grieving process.

DANNY: It is an important part of your work to experience this, because you are a teacher to so many who experience the same thing. You *have to* feel it in order to help other people work through their own grief. How could you possibly relate to bereaved parents if you said, "I have never felt guilt?"

Ten Steps for Opening a Conduit to the Higher Realms

1. Accept the idea that we exist in multiple dimensions at once and that we have an "earth self" and a "Heaven self." The goal of spiritual practice is to align these as much as possible. The soul knows exactly what will serve our growth and the growth of the whole, but the ego kicks and screams against it. The ego wants to live. The soul knows there is no death. <u>The ability to receive Divine communication is absolutely dependent on knowing and accepting this truth.</u>

2. Trust what you receive. This is the true definition of "faith." Practice via meditation, writing letters to yourself from the higher realms, talking with friends and sharing "psychic" experiences and developing a community of like-minded seekers. Support is vital, as is education. See the reading list at the back of this book.

3. Use visual tools. Imagine information printing on a computer screen, or a television or radio being turned on, or words being scrawled on paper. Or try to imagine that you're "downloading" words, pictures, images and phrases from your guides.

4. Work consistently on releasing blame, anger, judgment and helplessness. Do this by telepathically releasing people and ideas to which you are clinging. The more you release -- and the more gratitude you can realize for the growth lessons your soul created via these painful situations -- the more clearly you will hear the voice of God.

5. Write down or record everything you experience in dreams and meditation, even if you doubt what you're receiving. No exceptions!

6. Evidential information isn't necessary. You don't need flying tables, electrical disturbances or secrets that nobody else knows. You can *feel* when the connection happens. Trust that feeling.

7. Is it your imagination? The guides work with you, they never leave you, so even if you're "pretending" or using your "imagination," you're still summoning them, because the imagination realm *is* a higher realm. In using your imagination, you are opening up to a different kind of energy, and that's how channeling begins. Imagination is not a cop out. It's a first step. Do not disregard it. It's an opportunity to take a leap of faith.

8. There is only one question or prayer that is appropriate when working with the higher realms: *"What is the higher purpose of this experience? What am I in this situation to learn and how can I best use that lesson for my growth and the growth of all?"*

9. This work is about creating a shift, and it only takes a tiny shift in awareness to create a huge movement in your attitudes and energies, and that can change your life. Trust *implicitly* in signs, symbols, "coincidences," visions, intuitive impressions and dreams. The Divine is always trying to get your attention.

10. None of the above steps are optional.

7. The Gifts of Grief

"It would be so much easier to understand and accept death if we didn't see it as a loss."

Dr. Anna Noekeala Bonas

"Light and Darkness, life and death, right and left, are brothers of one another. They are inseparable. Because of this neither are the good good, nor evil evil, nor is life life, nor death death."

The Gospel of Phillip

Grief is like open-heart surgery. Nothing can rip us open, hurt us, scar us and heal us more than grief, and nothing brings us more valuable soul lessons. The primary gift of grief is that it changes us permanently and profoundly, and because we are never truly separated from those who have crossed over, their deaths invite us to enter new worlds along with them.

Grief cuts to the core of everything that defines us, and exposes places in our relationships, belief systems, family structures and social values that have been crying out for illumination and healing. Grief shakes us loose from our spiritual lethargy and creates an opening in us that is highly receptive to growth if we recognize the tools and choose to do the work. If we nurture that opening, if we honor it and work with it, stretching and strengthening it a little bit each day, we can discover previously unimagined worlds of wisdom and choose enlightenment over annihilation. Every one of us who's had a life-shattering grief experience has, on a soul level, asked grief to transform us, though on the ego/personality level, we are not aware of having made this request.

The finality and permanence of death is an illusion. Our energy simply hits a stopping point in the physical world the same way the car crashing off the cliff did in Chapter 1, and when it can go no further the energy is shifted into something else. The grief experience for a person who understands this can be vastly different than the grief experience for a person who doesn't. If we understand that our relationships continue after death, then that death cannot possibly be seen as a loss. It can only be seen as a change. Instead of saying "goodbye," we say, "Blessings to you on your journey. I'll see you again in a minute."

You're probably reading this book because you're interested in interdimensional communication and the afterlife. If your heart has been blasted open by grief in this lifetime (or in other lifetimes), then your interest in this material is no accident. It was written into your soul's curriculum, and what better way to master that course of study than to have someone on the Other Side with whom you'd desperately like to connect? That person's death, along with all the other growth plans it serves, provides you with the specific learning you requested. Remember, in Heaven there is no judgment. So at some point in time (though there *is* no time) you probably said to your soul family, "I would like to learn to communicate between dimensions." In response to this request, one or more members of your soul family happily volunteered to provide a death that would lead you to that knowledge. Or perhaps they agreed to help manifest an illness or accident in which you would have a near-death experience that changes your perspective and leads you toward metaphysical awareness.

Regardless of how it happens, your request to study interdimensional communications is being fulfilled. Recognizing that every experience is created in answer to the soul's desire for learning is the first step toward connecting grief with gratitude.

A NEW WAY OF LOOKING AT GRIEF AND LOSS

Imagine that a mother is crying about the death of her young daughter (we will call the daughter Jane). "She was so young! A compassionate, beautiful soul, pure, clean and perfect," the mother cries. "She loved unconditionally. She was completely innocent. Why did she have to die?"

There *is* an answer to the mother's question, though to understand it requires opening the senses to an elevated view of our purpose on earth. Jane's life, her earth personality, her soul, her death, everything she is and everything she does, is not separate from the rest of us. She is part of an enormous living organism called "Us." This is what the great teachers mean when they speak of Oneness. No one of Us is separate from any other of Us. When a piece of Us -- in this case a young girl named Jane -- moves into another dimension, it is never a personal affront against one of Us, nor is it a random, meaningless event, and it most certainly is never, *ever* a form of Divine punishment.

Jane's death, when viewed from the perspective of Us, is not a loss. It is simply a change of energy. Jane's life and death -- her soul's movement through this system -- is part of a much bigger picture that affects all of Us. Jane's death alters the lives of the people who knew her as well as thousands of interconnected, extended soul family members. The energy ripples out into the universe, and all of Us are transformed.

Imagine that Jane, her family, everybody who ever met her, everybody on earth, all beings in the higher realms and every spark of energy in the universe is like a fragment in the kaleidoscope we discussed in Chapter 4. When the slightest movement occurs, the fragments are rearranged. Jane's death, as well as every other action in the universe, moves the kaleidoscope, and the position of each fragment is shifted. No fragment stands alone. The piece of Us known as "Jane" in this lifetime is not separate from the rest of Us. Neither is your dog, a stranger on another continent or the person you perceive as your worst enemy. Healing and forgiveness, whether it's about grieving the death of a loved one or recovering from a childhood trauma, begins with this understanding.

In the kaleidoscope of Us, death is simply a shift that redistributes our positions, and in the process, moves us all forward in our awareness. On earth, on the ego level, these shifts cause great pain, but that pain teaches the most important spiritual lesson of all... that there is only US. When we see ourselves as part of the whole -- the way a finger or an eyelash is part of a body -- then we realize that our departed loved one is an eyelash on the body of US. When we can think and live as if we are part of something bigger than our individual earth identities, then we can accept these shifts with love and find peace and purpose in our lives. The alternative is to have an experience on earth of bitterness, blame, spiritual isolation, confusion and powerlessness. If that is the experience one chooses, then there is a purpose to that experience as well. There is never any judgment about these choices.

The ego sees itself as the center of the universe, and works tirelessly to maintain its illusion of control and separateness. When great trauma or loss occurs, there's a disruption in that system, and the ego fights frantically to survive and return to the status quo. Every time this happens, we have the opportunity to change our perceptions, move beyond the ego to a higher understanding and align more fully with the Divine. When tragedies can be recognized as opportunities, our experience on earth is much less difficult and much less ruled by fear and panic. When we need a reminder of this, we'll experience a tragedy or loss that stops the ego in its tracks and gives us a chance to listen to the soul instead. This is the whole purpose of incarnation… to remember that we're not separate from each other and not separate from God.

We do not toil alone.

A Word About my Own Grief Journey

It is said that the worst imaginable experience on earth is the death of a child. Millions of parents, myself included, have had this experience, and it leaves us asking, "Now that the worst has happened, what next?"

Losing a child can make us impervious to fear. Our worst fear has come true, and after that, there's not much that can hurt us. We are invincible. Laid off from a job? House in foreclosure? Do you or your spouse have a serious illness? We can laugh, albeit bitterly, in the face of adversity. We shout defiantly to the universe, "C'mon, what else ya got? Lay it on me. You can't hurt me anymore."

About 18 months after Danny died I realized that I had "died" with him. I was still physically alive and functioning somewhat normally, and there was a new life looming out ahead of me that seemed filled with promise and the potential for joy. I'd left a toxic marriage, moved 3000 miles away, bought a house and published a book. But I did it all while in an altered state that moved between numbness and hyper-awareness. I hadn't breathed or relaxed for one second during the ten years of Danny's illness, and now that the caregiving was over, I was still not breathing. I hadn't smiled, laughed, taken a day off, relaxed, played, loved, rested or exhaled in ten years. My heart was closed tight as a drum.

During a meditation one day, I had a vision that made an undeniable statement about one of my personal emotional issues. I saw a female monkey in a tree, cuddling her newborn baby, which was dead. She was petting it and comforting it, as if she was blessing it and sending on its way, and then she dropped it out of the tree onto the forest floor and swung through the trees, ready to move on. The image -- and its message -- was confusing to me. Was it telling me that I hadn't fully let go of my son, who'd been dead less than a year? Somehow that didn't feel like the right interpretation; it was too trite and too obvious. I knew there was more to it, so I asked my guides to help me. Over the next few days, in dreams and meditations, I received a more complex and on-target explanation than I could have come up with on my own or with a traditional therapist.

It wasn't about letting go of Danny. It was about changing the energy of *mothering*. I was 55 years old, so I would not be having any more children, and with my only child gone from physical existence, there would be no grandchildren. I had to look at the fact that mothering was the only kind of love I'd ever known how to give, but I'd used it inappropriately throughout my life by falling in love with lost, broken men and helping them get on their feet, only to have them leave me when their confidence was restored. I'd been misdirecting the energy of mother and healer for years, and if I wanted to grow and live again, I would have to find a new way to love. For me, in this incarnation's curriculum, the mothering energy in relationships has been a big issue.

"The monkey vision shows you an earthbound version of releasing. You saw a monkey because it represents humans, human life and human love, which is very limited compared to the love of Heaven. Many who come to you for teaching are mothers who have experienced the death of their children, and your work with them is a new, more appropriate outlet for the energy of mothering and healing. You created this new outlet through your experience with grief, and it is a great gift.

All relationships are acting out the one true relationship, the one true love, which is the Divine love that fuels all the energy in creation. Mothering is an essential element of that love, which is expressed as the Divine Mother in many of the world's religions. You are replacing your role as a physical mother on earth with a new role that is more like a priestess; a representative of the Divine Feminine, and in this role you hold the energy of "mother" for many mothers. You could not have stepped into this role without your unique grief experience. Your grief process is different than what most mothers experience, because you know that your child is still with you. Your commitment to teaching others that communication with Heaven is possible and that pain can be turned to light is a sacred agreement."

CLEARING YOUR HEART AND RELEASING PAIN

We never *recover* from grief, nor should we. Recovery suggests making something disappear, like a tumor or an addiction. The American Heritage Dictionary defines recovery as "restoring (oneself) to a normal state." Anybody who's grieved knows that we never return to the way we were before the experience. What we do instead is to integrate that experience into our lives, our personalities, our bodies and our souls.

Our immediate response to pain is to instinctively push it away. But with grief, instead of struggling to move away from the pain, true healing happens when we allow ourselves to move deeply and consciously *toward* it rather than away from it. But choosing to walk through it is difficult, especially in a society where death and grief makes people uncomfortable and we're constantly encouraged to "move on" and "let go." Many bereaved people quickly discover that they can't talk about their feelings with friends because the friends become visibly uneasy and don't know how to respond. The conversation -- and with it, the processing of our pain -- is quickly shut down and neatly wrapped up with trite comments like, "it's time to get on with your life." I've heard hundreds of stories about widows who are shunned by their married friends as if the death of a spouse is contagious, and this behavior is even more common when a child dies.

When we're grieving, we need our friends to listen to us and support us, but many bereaved people find that they end up supporting their friends instead by protecting them from the unpleasant story. The grief journey is a lonely one, which is why hospice bereavement groups and organizations like The Compassionate Friends are so valuable. They provide a social circle in which we can speak freely and in detail about what we've experienced without fear of upsetting or offending anyone. We'll talk more about that in the next chapter.

If you're grieving alone, what resources are available to you beyond support groups and grief therapy? What can you do in your darkest hours, when you're alone in your bed missing the partner who once slept beside you, or crying in the supermarket when you walk past the aisle where you used to buy your child's favorite foods?

There is only one true source of comfort, and it can be found by reaching out to the higher realms. When our hearts have been hibernating in a dark room with the curtains closed for months or years, at some point, if we are going to heal, it is necessary to allow the light back in, and this can only be done by accessing our conduit to Heaven. Sometimes we're so busy being functional as humans that we don't realize how much pain we are carrying. As we go through the years experiencing life's various disappointments, wounds and losses, we keep adding new layers of insulation to shore us up and keep us going. Many of us hold ourselves in this state for decades without even knowing it, and grief is often the trigger that pushes us to a higher perspective where we can be more open to love and peace.

The following meditations are designed to clear the heart and help you connect to the essence of your loved one(s) on The Other Side. If you've practiced the exercise for opening a conduit on page 106, you will be ready to try some of these. The most important thing to remember is to accept every image, symbol or word that comes to you, even if you think it's just your imagination. These practices will not only help with your grief by showing you that your loved ones are still very close by, they will also help you establish a relationship with the higher realms in general, where there are guides, angels and teachers waiting to assist

PRACTICES AND MEDITATIONS

A beginner's meditation for connecting with a loved one

I originally designed this meditation for children in the hope that I could use it at the children's grief camp run by our local hospice. The words are simple, gentle and appropriate for a very young person, which is why it's perfect for beginners:

Close your eyes and breathe very slowly for a few seconds, and begin to count each breath. Breathe in, counting to three or four or whatever is comfortable for you. When you breathe out, do the same. Find a comfortable, easy rhythm that relaxes you.

Now, imagine that every time you inhale you are breathing zillions of tiny stars of all different colors, like rainbow stardust. Every time you inhale, these stars go inside you and fill you up with beautiful, colored light. And when you exhale, you blow them all out again. Breathe them in, hold them inside you for a few seconds, and then blow them out. This light and energy of these stars is filling you with light.

As you continue to breathe, become aware that you are breathing pure, light energy. It's the energy of everything in the universe, especially LOVE. It's the energy of all the people you love, and everything that exists... animals, trees, planets, feelings and ideas, bodies, spirits... everything. As you breathe this energy in and out you will know that you're connected to this energy all the time, and that you can never be separated from it, no matter what. And you can never be separated from anybody else either, because we're all made of this same stardust. It connects us, whether we're in this world or another one.

Now think about the person or people you love that have died. Can you see them standing there, surrounded by the beautiful stardust light? Focus on this image, just use your imagination and place that person there, and take a few moments to just breathe and feel their presence. Imagine them smiling at you, radiating love. If you lose focus, don't worry, just use your imagination to bring them back, and cover them with this colored stardust. Cover yourself with it too, and allow it to connect you to your loved one, so that you are together in the light of love.

What you're feeling right now may feel a little sad, but it also feels like love, doesn't it? Stay in that feeling and know that you are never really separated from this person. The energy of love is stronger than anything, stronger than life or death. It lives on forever, it never dies.

If you like, imagine that this person is speaking to you. What are they saying? You can also speak to them. In your mind, send a message, whatever you want to say, just imagine that they hear you. Take a moment to do this, and keep breathing the light in and out.

You will always be connected like this, and if you practice this meditation on your own, the connection will get even stronger. You can do this any time you want to because the love that connects you is always there. The person you love, the person you've lost, is not really lost at all. You can find them here, in your heart, any time.

Now focus on your breathing for a moment, tell the person that you're going to leave now, but you'll be back very soon, and thank them for making this connection. When you're ready, open your eyes and come back here, back to this room. Take as much time as you need.

Breathing with a loved one on the other side

This is a more advanced meditation that is particularly powerful if you were present when your loved one took his or her last breath. I received this meditation from Danny two years after his death, on a day when I was having vivid memories of his labored breathing during the last 24 hours of his life. I could not get the breathing image out of my mind for days, and I wondered why it was coming through so strongly.

Whenever I feel something like this, I go into meditation to seek an explanation, because I can sense that my guides are trying to tell me something. In this case, Danny wanted to give me this exercise for establishing a stronger connection with him. I quite frequently sense him standing behind me, and I've heard that many people experience the same thing when their departed loved ones are present... a sense of someone behind them, or a tickling on their backs. Many mediums, when doing readings, see the departed standing behind the client.

Begin, as usual, by breathing deeply and counting your breaths until you can feel your body relax completely. The focus on breath is extremely important here.

As you breathe, imagine that your loved one has appeared behind you. Feel the energy of their presence, and imagine that each of your breaths draws them closer to you, until you feel your loved one's chest pressed against your back. Your loved one has come to help you establish a connection via your breath. As you breathe more and more deeply, be aware that your breath is circulating through both bodies... your physical body and your loved one's astral body. You are breathing together, as if the breath is moving from your lungs to your loved one's and back again, synchronizing until you are breathing as one. Remain in this very deep, connected place for as long as you like, simply breathing with your loved one. It is a very strong connection, and you will sense a lifting up, a euphoric feeling, as you link to the higher energies through the breath connection. This is very real. You may simply stay and breathe with your loved one, feeling their love and their presence. Receive any verbal or symbolic messages your loved one may be sending, or simply bask in their love.

Here is a variation on this meditation, if you'd like to take it a step further:

You will now begin to sense that there are many other beings standing behind your loved one... a parade of guides, teachers and ancestors, lined up together and breathing in synchronization with you. This is an expression of oneness, of your deep connection with all the beings and all the energies in the higher realms. As you continue to breathe with your Heavenly companions, you can begin to feel the pulsing and breathing of the earth, and the deeper you breathe, the bigger your consciousness becomes, until you are breathing in synch with the solar systems and the entire universe. Stay in that place for as long as you like, simply breathing, with your loved one as your link. You are experiencing an infusion of healing love that carries you Home.

THE DOLPHIN MEDITATION

This is an even deeper version of breathing with a loved on the Other Side that will actually allow you to follow him or her to Heaven. It requires a lot of peace and concentration and is quite lengthy and detailed, so it is best done with a friend who can read it out loud and guide you through the steps. As an option, you can record yourself reading it, and then play it back as a guided meditation. It's even more effective with music (I like to use a piece called "Tibetan Plateau" by David Parsons). It's a wonderful exercise that will take you deep into the 6th and 7th chakras.

Begin, as usual, with deep breathing. Imagine that your body is an outline, like a pencil drawing on white paper, outlining the perimeter of your form. Beginning at your feet, slowly begin to erase the outline, as if with a giant eraser. See your feet beginning to disappear, and then your knees, slowly, as you breathe more and more deeply. With each exhale breath, imagine more of your body is disappearing. Breathe deeply into your solar plexus area as you imagine it disappearing, and then your chest, your neck, your head, until the outline is completely gone and the paper is now blank.

Now bring into your imagination a loved one on The Other Side (I will refer to this person as "your beloved"). Call your beloved to you now, and see him or her standing in front of you, looking into your eyes. You may feel a lot of emotion when this happens, so allow those feelings to flow freely. To find peace and maintain focus, always return to your breathing.

Look deeply into the eyes of your beloved, and see them breathing, slowly, in an out, and notice that they are synchronizing their breath with yours. Stare deeply into their eyes and begin breathing with them, eyes locked, breathing together. This alignment will allow you to follow your beloved to the higher realms. You are raising your frequency to meet theirs, and your breath is being translated into light. Breath on earth becomes light in Heaven.

Your beloved is now leading you to a beautiful, deserted beach, where there is nothing but the two of you and the sand, the water and the breeze, gently pulsing with the flowing pattern of breath that you are now sharing.

He or she is leading you gently into water, and you realize with delight that your beloved has taken on the form of a dolphin, beckoning you to come into the water, which is warm and safe. Put your arms around the dolphin and let it carry you into the deep blue, knowing that you will be safely returned to the beach after your journey. You can breathe easily in this water, and that you are completely safe, sharing the breath and light of the dolphin. Deeper and deeper into the water you are lovingly carried, and you have never felt so safe and so loved before. You are being taken to a place where you can see and communicate with beings in the higher realms, including the loved one who is leading you there now. You are being taken HOME.

Your doubts and fears are left behind on the beach, on earth. Here, in this higher place, you are in complete safety, and can completely trust all that you see and experience, because you know it is from the light, and there is no fear. You are traveling into deepening layers of blue, feeling more relaxed, safe and comfortable than you have ever felt before. You are safe in the arms of love. In this very magical realm, your beloved and you will find a common language with which to communicate. It may not be in words, but may be in thoughts transmitted telepathically. Perhaps your beloved will show you around, will show you images from the realm in which he or she lives, or may show images from your own life, or from some future life. He or she may give you an object or show you a symbol, which is often the way in which communication from the higher realms is given. It does not necessarily have to be words. Breathe the breath of your beloved, just stay and breathe, nothing more. With each breath, you will hear, or feel or sense a message. Trust what you're hearing, allow it to be true.

When you are ready, begin your return journey. The dolphin will now carry you back up through the water, through the lighter and lighter shades of blue, lighter and lighter as you see the sunlight at the surface of the water. You gently break through the surface, and see the shoreline waiting for you. You have been carried back to shore, and the dolphin now resumes the form of your beloved. Look into his or her eyes and breathe together for a few moments to stabilize and ground you as you return to earth. Listen to what he or she is saying... *You can meet me here any time you want. I am always with you. We are never separated. I will always be here to guide you, as will others in the higher realms. You are safe and loved and guided.*

And now release your beloved, say goodbye for the moment, because you will meet again, on this beach, anytime you wish. Feel the peace of knowing that you can always connect like this and that your beloved is always near.

Writing a Letter From Heaven

This is an exercise in "channeled writing." Even if you've never tried to listen to messages from the higher realms, this exercise may begin to open that door. The hardest part is allowing yourself to come to a place of absolute trust in what you receive. It might take a few minutes or it might take a few years. We're not talking about partial trust. The trust has to be *absolute.* You have to leave behind your mind, your beliefs, your ego, your expectations and even your intentions. All you have to do is *receive.*

Before you begin, say a little prayer asking for the conduit to be opened. Breathe deeply and relax. Ask your guides to assist you. The moment you ask, they will arrive.

1. Sit down with paper and pen (or at your computer) and write "Dear (your name)." You may focus on a loved one on the Other Side if you wish, or you can ask for messages from guides or angels.

2. Start writing. Write anything at all. You will immediately feel self-conscious and foolish and say to yourself, "This is stupid. This is just me talking to myself. I'm just writing what I think I'm supposed to hear." That's OK. Everybody thinks that at first. Just keep writing. Don't stop.

3. Write everything that comes into your mind, no matter how irrelevant it seems. Are you seeing an image of a baseball? Write to yourself about it. Say, "Here is a baseball for you to see." Follow that train of thought as far and long as you can. *Someone is sending that image to you.* Are you hearing words or phrases? Write them down, no matter how silly they may seem. *Someone is sending these messages.*

4. The only thing that will stop you from receiving is your own doubts. You will stop yourself a hundred times during this process to indulge your doubts, fears and rationalizations, and that's OK. Just keep going. Guides and loved ones in the higher realms make an effort to reach us, and our doubts create interference. They need our participation in order to reach us. Ask your guides to help remove your doubts.

5. Do this exercise only for as long as you're comfortable and can concentrate. When it starts to feel forced, it's time to stop. You might be able to do this for ten minutes or ten seconds. If you sincerely want to make contact, keep trying and eventually you will have success.

6. Sometimes we receive very clear verbal messages... pages and pages of words. And sometimes we receive symbolic messages, like a baseball or a song. Write them all down and don't worry if they don't immediately make sense to you. You can analyze them later. If you receive these things with an open mind and an open heart, they will eventually begin to tell a story.

7. You will know that you're receiving transmissions from The Divine because the words, the writing, the feeling, the energy, will not feel like YOU. It will become automatic. It will flow freely and easily, because you've taken your fear, ego and personality out of the way. You will absolutely recognize this feeling when it comes. For some people it happens in seconds. For others it can take years.

8. Don't give up. This is your birthright.

8. The Politics of Bereavement

"… Society polices grief; it controls and instructs the bereaved about how to think, feel, and behave. All societies have rules about how the emotions of grief are to be displayed and handled. In some cultures, for example, those who grieve should talk to the dead, and in other cultures the name of the dead should never be spoken. Those who do not conform to the social expectations are labeled aberrant. In contemporary psychotherapeutic culture, aberrant grief is deemed pathological. In other cultures the labels would be different—counter-revolutionary in communist cultures, sinful or idolatrous in monotheistic religions." [19]

The Encyclopedia of Death and Dying

"Grieving is one of many channels through which we find our way to Oneness. Grief helps us remember our spiritual home, and in grief, we are forced to live in our hearts, which carries us back to Source if we allow it to."

Danny

In comparison to many who work in the field of death, dying and bereavement, I'm still a novice. At this writing, I've been a hospice volunteer for three years and have been facilitating workshops, writing books and counseling people on afterlife awareness for about the same amount of time. It's a drop in the bucket. But I've been metaphysically-minded since adolescence, when I first developed my voracious appetite for information about religion and spirituality. During those years I read everything I could get my hands on, including the Tibetan Book of the Dead, which made an irreversible impression on my psyche and my soul.

---

[19] The Encyclopedia of Death and Dying - http://www.deathreference.com/Gi-Ho/Grief-and-Mourning-in-Cross-Cultural-Perspective.html

The Tibetan Book of the Dead is what is known as "funerary literature," which means it's written for the express purpose of guiding a dying or newly-dead person through their initial entry to the afterlife. In traditional practice the text is read out loud to a dying person or over the body of a newly-deceased person. The practice of guiding a soul on its journey from the physical to the non-physical is sacred and precious, and in many cultures, to many people (including myself), witnessing a death is as beautiful and profound as witnessing a birth.

The concept of bonding with a baby in the womb by singing to it, reading poetry to it, playing soothing music to it and even teaching the baby a foreign language in vitro, echoes the idea of guiding someone from one realm into another. The idea of womb-to-earth guidance became wildly popular around the time that my generation (baby boomers) began having its own babies, but the idea of providing guidance at the other end of life, when we're leaving earth for our next destination, is still pretty much unthinkable in America.

How can we hope to introduce the idea of conscious dying if death is denied, sanitized and closeted, and a non-judgmental afterlife is loudly disclaimed? The common rationalization is that we can *see* a person die, but we can't see where he or she goes next, so there's no point in addressing something that we cannot see or prove. But when you consider that millions of average people have near-death experiences, deathbed visitations from angels or ancestors and evidential psychic experiences with the departed, denying this aspect of existence deprives us of a legitimate and rightful piece of the human experience.

In 2007 I began speaking to various groups around the country that had an interest in a mystical perspective of death and the afterlife. It was an eclectic audience, made up of churches, metaphysical study circles, grief recovery groups, bookstores and an occasional hospice. I was bursting with excitement about bringing my message to people who were seeking outside-the-box answers. My presentations were met with overwhelming support and enthusiasm.

In 2009, with one published book under my belt and another on the way, I expanded my reach to international symposiums on death and dying, hospice seminars and national conferences for the leading grief groups in the U.S. With innocent optimism, I sent countless proposals to countless conference organizers, and was utterly astonished to discover that while many of these professionals were brilliant and accomplished at walking up to death's door, few were willing to walk *through* it.

There are two well-respected bereavement groups in the U.S. that do excellent work helping parents who've experienced the death of a child. Being such a parent myself, I approached both of these groups to ask for consideration as a speaker at one of their upcoming conferences. Although I'd spoken to some of the small, local chapters of these groups and was warmly received, I had a completely different experience when I approached the same groups on the *national* level.

Here are some of their responses to my workshop proposal (the names have been deleted out of respect for the organizations and their members):

Dear Terri,

As [xxx] Special Projects Coordinator, I am charged with selecting the presenters at the national conferences. Our 31 past conferences have taught us that--while we welcome a wide diversity of viewpoints--controversial topics such as channeling are to be avoided. We do not ever wish to erect barriers for the newly bereaved. Unfortunately, therefore, I would have to decline your proposal for future conferences.

Dear Terri,

The [xxx] organization is designed to offer hope, friendship, and understanding to bereaved family members following the death of a child. This is accomplished by allowing our membership to share their grief and pain in a warm, loving environment... As an organization, as officials of chapters, and representatives of the umbrella organization, we must walk the fine line to make sure ALL parents feel the love and warmth of a caring environment no matter what their religion, racial or ethnic background or economic circumstances or beliefs.

Dear Terri,

As a bereaved parent myself, I am familiar with some of the unusual experiences that many bereaved parents relate, and have had such experiences myself.

[xxx]'s policy regarding this issue is based upon the belief that those who seek metaphysical counsel need to do so individually and privately. As a national organization, [xxx] has chosen not to sponsor this activity.

Erect barriers for the newly bereaved? Racial or ethnic background or economic circumstances? These statements baffled me, but this one took the prize:

"... all chapter-sponsored events should strive to make the atmosphere 'inclusive,' warm, and inviting for all members regardless of their beliefs. While some members may find a degree of comfort in the notion that they can receive a communication from their dead child, others will be very disturbed."

That doesn't sound very "inclusive" to me. What about the people who "may find a degree of comfort that they can receive a communication from their dead child?" Why are they *not* included? What's truly disturbing here is that these groups are not giving their members a choice about what they want to hear.

I once gave a talk at a *regional* (as opposed to *national*) conference for one of these groups (at the local level the organizers have more autonomy, so they can actually *be* inclusive if they choose to). At this event, the conference organizer was skilled at meeting planning and scheduled my workshop as a breakout session at the same time as two other workshops. This way the attendees could choose which workshop they wanted to attend in that particular time slot. The other workshop presenters ended up addressing rooms full of empty chairs while my workshop had a full house.

In another speaking engagement for another local chapter of the same group, I made a point of being cautious about going too far into the woo-woo zone with information on after-death communication. I knew the organization was somewhat skittish about this topic, so I erred on the side of caution. Even though I'd been promoted as an after-death communicator, I kept to the safer topics of grieving and preparation for the death of a loved one.

During the Q & A period, a woman said, "I'd like to hear more after-death communication." The other people chimed in with the same request. The organizer nodded her head in agreement and indicated that we had extra time, so I led the group in a guided meditation to help them connect with their children on the other side. Afterwards, the audience members came to me, one by one, thanking me profusely while telling me their grief stories and sobbing in gratitude.

People *want* this information. Not all of them, certainly. But enough to warrant a breakout session at a national conference. Who has the right to deny this to them? I have some experience with conference and event planning myself, and one of the basic tenets is to give people a choice of at least two topics in any given time slot. Most well-planned conferences end by giving attendees a feedback form to help organizers plan the following year's conference. For these groups, such a form should look something like this:

What would you like to see in future conferences? Check one or more:

1. Panel of medical experts talking about physical death
2. Bereaved individuals talking about their experiences
3. Private sessions with grief counselors
4. Information on after-death communication and psychic phenomena
5. More teddy bears, doilies, picture frames and other junk for sale

---

OK, maybe I'm being a little hostile in item # 5. But you get the idea. Part of the problem is that this topic is considered *religious,* and when wading in religious waters, fear runs deep. I suppose if they let me do a presentation on after death communication, they'd have to also let an evangelical Christian do a seminar called "Did Your Child go to Hell for Committing Suicide?" There are probably people who'd want to attend such a presentation, and if we're being inclusive, then why exclude them? Why not have a whole section at a conference on spirituality, with all the various flavors represented? After all, we're talking about death here, which is something that cannot be seen or understood with the five physical senses, so how can it not be spiritual? But in the name of political correctness, spirituality is pretty much neglected by many hospice and grief recovery programs.

I once spoke to a chapter of this same group in the deep south, and 70% of conference attendees signed up for my workshop (in the bible belt!). They did the guided meditation. They cried. The bought my book. They hugged me. They filled out feedback forms that gave my talk a 100% positive response. The only comments they added to the form, "The presentation should have been longer," and "This was the best workshop of the weekend." But the national leadership of this group, despite these glowing reports, still refuses to let me -- and other experts in my field -- speak on metaphysical topics.

Which brings me to the bridge I'm trying to construct between bereavement and politics.

I am a one-woman cheering section for the advancement of hospice and palliative care in America. I'm completely enamored with the idea of hospice, the practice of hospice care, the professionals who work in the field, and of course, the patients and their families. Hospice workers, perhaps second only to Buddhist priests, are among the most compassionate people on earth when it comes to dealing with death. They do this work for *love,* and most of them came to this work as a result of their own personal grief journeys and their desire to help others make that journey in the most peaceful way possible. It is an elevated spiritual calling.

The people who buy my books, attend my seminars and come to me for counseling are genuinely interested in birth, death and the journey of the soul, and they are very open and willing to explore new territory. I've been asked in media interviews if I ever encounter people who are afraid of what I teach, and when I examine this question, I have to answer honestly that the professionals in medical, hospice and religious communities are usually the most fearful.

In Chapter Four I mentioned the children's grief camp run by a local hospice where I volunteered for two summers. I ended up resigning from that hospice under pressure from the bereavement coordinator (we'll call her Denise), who told me that she was afraid of me and didn't want me in her upcoming training session because I might ask questions she couldn't answer. She'd assembled a long list of absurd reasons why I didn't make a suitable hospice worker, but added, "your patients adore you." The real problem? I was well-known in the community as an intuitive and spiritual teacher, and she didn't want that sort of thing associated with her hospice.

At grief camp, children who've lost a loved one can attend, free of charge, and spend a weekend with loving, attentive, trained hospice volunteers who lead the children in games and processes to help them deal with their losses. A lot of the activities at camp are rituals to help the kids get in touch with grief, to face it, feel it and talk about it. For many of these kids, our camp was the first chance they ever had to talk about their feelings and express their grief openly.

In a previous year I'd asked Denise if I could conduct a special guided meditation for the kids at camp. I'd learned this meditation from a hospice counselor in Arizona who specialized in helping children cope with grief. It's a remarkable meditation in which you imagine that your departed loved one is standing in front of you, looking into your eyes, synchronizing his/her breathing with yours. This is the first step in allowing your heart to open and sensing the love that connects you, even between worlds (you'll find it in Chapter Seven: *"A Beginners Meditation for Connecting With a Loved One"*).

In order to demonstrate this to Denise, I sat with her in her office and guided her through the meditation. When it was over, she was moved to tears, and said she'd think about whether or not to let me use it with the kids at camp. A year later she was still thinking about it, and when I pressed her for an answer, she said something remarkably similar to what the national grief groups said: *It's too spiritual. It will alienate or anger people with conflicting religious beliefs.*

There is nothing religious in that meditation. So where, exactly, is the affront here?

My guides have explained to me that connecting with other dimensions, even in visualization or imagination, challenges the beliefs and boundaries that make people feel secure on earth. The ego/personality wants to be in control of its world, and in order to maintain that control, the world has to be small enough to be manageable. Introducing other worlds is like walking someone to the edge of a cliff and asking them to jump off. The structures of western religion and culture, even with the fear it instills, creates a sense of safety and belonging. The ego knows exactly what it can and cannot do. We believe in prescribed ideas, and it isn't safe to venture beyond those ideas because new ideas come from "them" and the only place we can be safe is with "us." The world of "us," in the ego's view, is the safest place to live, and jumping off a cliff is not recommended if we want to stay safe.

With an infantile view of God as a protective parent that keeps us from being exposed to dangerous or challenging circumstances, we are not given a natural chance to grow. We all know that as children grow, they venture farther and farther from their parents in their quest for independence and experience. A parent who would not allow a child this freedom would be considered neurotic or even dangerous. Yet there are many people who believe that God does not want his children to explore their connection to higher realms.

BEREAVEMENT ETIQUETTE

I'm normally an outgoing, very verbal person who is comfortable with emotional exposure, but during the first two years after my son's death I went into radio silence in terms of sharing my true feelings with people. I'd moved to a new town and made new friends, but they knew a different *me*... the A.D. (After Danny) version of me, and I barely knew that person myself. I could talk to them about my divorce or the other little dramas in my life, all of which were safe topics that anybody could relate to. But the subject of my son's death was so taboo and unspeakable that I barely mentioned it. People were comfortable as long as they felt that I was doing fine and putting the "tragic" event behind me.

In deep grief we suffer alone. Death is so untouchable in our culture that the bereaved themselves become untouchable. Bereaved people often experience being shunned by their social groups, family members and colleagues soon after a death occurs. Our society is sorely lacking in etiquette guidelines for dealing with death and bereavement, so the preferred method is usually to sweep it aside as quickly as possible. The standard for bereavement leave in American companies is only three days, after which we're expected to get back to work and back to normal. The less attention drawn to our grief the better, because our grief makes people uncomfortable. While friends and family members may gather to bring food, help with funeral arrangements and offer condolences for the first days or weeks after a death, many of the bereaved find that after the calls and cards stop coming, nobody speaks of the event again. One of the greatest gifts we can give to someone who's lost a loved one is to stay in touch and speak of the departed a year later, two years later, five years later and beyond. But sadly, within a month or two, our grief is neatly tucked away and forgotten by most of our friends and family members.

As children, we are taught how to behave in a museum, at a birthday party or in a classroom at school. We're taught how to speak respectfully to our elders, how to say *please* and *thank you* and how to act appropriately in various social situations. But nobody teaches us how to behave around death.

I once had a client with whom I worked for several years. He became a dear friend and spent a lot of time with my family, frequently joining us for holiday dinners and backyard barbecues. He was like an uncle to Danny, but didn't come to Danny's funeral and never said a word to me about Danny's death. We just carried on our business relationship as if nothing had happened. In the same vein, a widow once told me that her husband died of a heart attack while playing golf with his friend. The traumatized friend didn't come to the funeral and was not heard from until more than a year later. Similarly, many bereaved parents find themselves ignored on Mothers Day, Fathers Day or the child's birthday, even though they would cherish some support and acknowledgment on these important dates. It's also common for the friends and family of bereaved parents to avoid talking about their own children for fear of triggering pain and envy in the parent who has lost a child.

It's understandable that we would be uncomfortable about the death of a child or someone who dies tragically, because it brings home the reality that none of us is ever truly safe from harm and we're all potentially vulnerable to such a fate. But why shy away from the death of an elderly person who was seriously ill, for whom death is a natural, expected event? In my mother's social circle of widows in their 70s and 80s, it's not unusual for their married friends to stop socializing with them once they're widowed. The widows form their own social networks and become excellent support for one another, but they're acutely aware that they've been shut out by the couples who were once their closest friends.

I hear stories like this all the time. Is this is a behavior peculiar to modern America? Is it different in Australia or England? Is it human nature, or is it culturally programmed? Does it vary between different social structures or communities? Do African Americans deal with death differently that American white people? Do Catholics behave differently than Jews? Do poor people respond to death differently than rich people?

My friend Mukesh Chaturvedi is a writer and attorney in India who recently wrote this fascinating description of how death is handled by traditional Hindus:

"Helping a family when a death occurs is both a spiritual and social duty. There are no professional undertakers here, so it is the family's task to care for the body and the cremation. For the first 13 days there are continuous ceremonies. The responsible family member, usually the eldest son, performs the last rites, which includes lighting the pyre, and during those 13 days he will be somewhat of a hermit while relatives care for the rest of the family. Women cry a lot, and are encouraged to do so. On the 13th day, there is a feast, and religious ceremonies can continue for up to a year. Many marriages are arranged during this period because the community is so tightly massed together.

"The death of very old people is always celebrated, and people start planning the feast immediately. Death is accepted, understood and honored here. Lots of what people say on such occasions reflects the philosophy of the Bhagavad Gita [sacred Hindu scriptures]. They say, " He is not dead, he has only left his earthly body behind.

132

"Perhaps you know of this Islamic tradition... if you meet a janaza (a funeral procession with people carrying a coffin), you are supposed to walk alongside it or help carry it for at least 40 steps."

What a beautiful tradition! Not only are Muslims required to stop what they're doing to honor the passing coffin, they are required to walk alongside it, to be part of it, and allow it to be part of them. It's an excellent way to personally and publicly embrace death without fear or repulsion.

Odani Keiko, a Japanese journalist, told me that dying in Japan has been increasingly handled quietly and covertly in hospitals, but there are still strict social conventions related to honoring the dead, attending funerals and maintaining relationships after a death. It would be unthinkable to avoid a funeral or leave a social circle just because somebody has died.

"The Japanese are not burdened with guilt about facing God, so perhaps this makes the concept of an afterlife easier to accept," Odani says. "It's believed that human souls still live after death and come visit the family in mid-summer. I still remember the old days when people made animals out of cucumbers eggplants and sticks and put them on streets to greet the return of the dead. The dead are clearly more loved than feared."

George Bonano, a professor of clinical psychology at Columbia University whose work focuses on coping with grief and trauma, recently conducted a study comparing grief processing in the U.S. and China. Dr. Bonano noted that the focus of grief in western countries is mainly on accepting the *finality* of death, so western grieving is very much about breaking bonds with the loved one. By contrast, in China it is believed that the person isn't really gone, and there are rituals and behaviors designed to acknowledge the continued presence of the departed.[20]

"They have a responsibility to help the dead person on his journey," Dr. Bonano says. "Because of this belief, the sense of loss isn't as important as working with the dead to help them find their

---

[20] http://www.tc.columbia.edu/news/article.htm?id=5433

way. This task helps people feel connected, so grief is much easier to deal with. Some of these practices include cleaning the grave regularly, bringing offerings of food and burning paper replicas of everyday objects that the dead might need in the afterlife, such as shoes or pots The most common paper offering is paper money. In cemeteries and ancestral halls, the Chinese literally burn bags of paper money, which they send as offerings to deceased loved ones."

While most of us can't imagine burning bags of symbolic money, the idea of "afterlife care" links the world of the dead with the world of the living in a way that blurs the boundaries between us and expands our view of existence. Can you imagine how different bereavement would be if our culture supported us in maintaining an after-death connection? And if we could learn how to be consciously and fearlessly involved in the dying process -- for ourselves and for others -- the whole circle of birth, death, dying and the afterlife could be approached with eyes and hearts wide open.

9. I Can See Home From Here

"No path home is better than any other path. All paths take you there, because all it takes to get there is true desire, a pure, open heart and faith that God has no reason to say, 'No, you may not be with me.' to any person for any reason."

Neale Donald Walsch

Everybody - no exceptions -- "makes it" to Heaven. One of the most absurd and unnecessary misconceptions we have is that some people go to Heaven and others don't.

After Danny died we kept his body at home for five hours before we called the mortuary to take it away. During that time many of our closest friends came to visit, and they included our neighbors, a missionary couple who frequently traveled to Africa to convert tribal people to Christianity. They happened to have, at that time, one of the African women staying with them as a houseguest for an extended visit. The woman barely spoke English, but she came to my house and said a beautiful prayer over Danny's body... a gorgeous, rhythmic, singsong prayer in her language that melted my heart. When she was finished and I asked her what the words meant, she said, "it was asking God to please allow his soul into Heaven."

I was jolted out of my enchantment. Why would anybody have to ask for entrance into the higher realms?

Everybody goes to Heaven. The idea that we have to beg for Divine Love perpetrates the myth that we don't already have it.

DEATH IS A MIRACLE

People say birth is a miracle because the system through which we come to earth through each other's bodies is truly miraculous. But death is an equivalent miracle. In order for the cycle of birth/reincarnation/death to continue, there has to be a revolving door, a system of ingress and egress. It is a complex system, and my guides can describe it much better than I can:

"There is great labor in death, as in birth. It is not easy to die *or* to be born. It's a very long journey that cannot be measured in space or time, because it is a journey between dimensions. Before birth, the soul does not occupy the body, but is *remotely* attached, in a similar way that we are attached to you across dimensions. The soul knows that it has chosen that body, and so it's involved in the growth and nurturing of the fetus. Plans are made for that body before conception, before incarnation, about how it will be formed, whether or not it will be born, if it will be healthy or sick, whether the mother will survive childbirth and other issues related to the soul's plan for that incarnation.

The soul is in a supervisory role, working in concert with the souls of the mother, father, siblings and others affected by the life of the soul about to be born. The body itself is on autopilot, focusing only on being formed, supported by the souls around it. It does not require the soul to be *inside* the body in a physical sense. The body is operated by remote control in a sense, until it is born, at which time it is required that the soul be completely integrated with it. The soul does not necessarily live "inside" the body in a physical sense, but is inside and outside at the same time, moving freely between the dimensions. This can't really be explained or measured in physical terms like "inside" or "outside." The soul (or soul family team) supervises the development of the body during gestation, but once the body takes its first breath, the soul becomes integrated, and cannot separate *completely* again until death. It can separate in a limited way, journeying away from the body through dreams, meditation, our-of-body or near-death experiences, but it is always connected by something that could best be described as a luminous fiber.

Dying is a mirror image of the remote relationship between the soul and the body during the conception, gestation and birth process. When a person is dying, the soul begins to separate, and sort of rewinds in the opposite direction of what it did during the birth phase. The soul starts moving toward the supervisory position again, toward remote control, peeling away from the

136

indelible connection it had to the body during physical life. The soul starts to move back to the remote location, which is of course not a physical location in space, but a different dimension of vibration. When a person dies slowly, this process of gradual separation is very observable.

When a person dies instantly, the same thing happens, but it is not as observable. This is a good illustration of the meaning of "metaphysical," in the sense that activity can be happening on more than one plane simultaneously and there is a bridge that connects the physical and non-physical worlds. When somebody dies instantly, the intention for that death has already been put into motion. The soul begins to separate from the body, hours, days or weeks before the event, because the soul knows its own intention and is already in the process of manifesting that intention. The body -- or the personality/ego -- is usually not aware of this, but that's not always the case. Sometimes there *is* awareness of an impending death.

You've heard about people who pay off their bills, call old friends to say hello and put their affairs in order a few weeks before dying in a plane crash. It is a subtle knowing... most of the time the person is not consciously aware of this. People on the Other Side who died suddenly, would tell you of a subtle shift in their awareness or their behaviors in the hours, days or weeks prior to the death. All deaths, as with all births, are by agreement. When a soldier dies in a war, the person who killed him, the people who witnessed his death, his family members and the leaders of the governments sponsoring the war are part of an alignment of persons, places and events that lead to that death, in a ripple effect. All these energies are aligning their intention for that moment, for a specific purpose... the expansion and growth of the souls involved.

After death, the work of our souls continues on the higher planes. Growth is still occurring, but at a higher frequency. At this level we are free from the judgments, fears and the constraints of the ego, so the work is done more efficiently, fueled by pure love.

There are many helpers who assist in offering light, love and healing to the arrivals. Some beings have issues of resistance to work on, and they bring those issues with them. Many souls come in with anger and sadness and grief, but these states are being healed and transformed constantly at different speeds for different people. We can learn and grow at whatever pace we choose, whatever fits with the plan we're creating for ourselves. There is no judgment about these states, because it is all love here, everybody is welcomed and healed as needed for their soul's path."

WORKING WITH THE DYING

When the soul has made the decision to depart, whether death is immediately imminent or months away, the work that goes on in other dimensions has already begun. The person's consciousness becomes more open and receptive, and in this state the soul can easily receive telepathic communication and spiritual guidance. If you are working with the dying, your guides and the guides of the dying person will assist you. They are closer than ever at this time, and your love for the dying person, along with your unconditional trust in Spirit will automatically bring in their help. When the heart is open, the teachers perk up their ears and pay attention.

Just as meditation, dreams and prayer open a conduit to the Divine, so does the process of dying. It is a time in which enormous infusions of light can come through. If you are witnessing or assisting with a death, whether you're a friend, caregiver, priest or paramedic, creating an energetic field of love and fearlessness is the greatest contribution you can make. There is no greater gift for the dying than to be introduced to the vast love available in the higher realms.

But it is not always possible to hold a dying person's hand and lead him in a guided visualization with soothing words, soft music, candles and prayers. In fact, most people do *not* die this way. Hospice workers report that people who die with their loved ones nearby frequently choose to take their final breath when the friends or family members are out of the room, because the energy of grief, sadness and attachment makes it difficult for the dying person to let go. One hospice nurse told me, "A dying person surrounded by loved ones is like the guest of honor at a big party. It's not polite to be the first to leave."

People die alone and afraid on battlefields, in car wrecks, earthquakes and hospital emergency rooms every day. What comfort or assistance is available to them? If their only preparation for death is what they've absorbed from fear-based religious teachings, then death is likely to be terrifying (though they will be met with massive doses of healing love when they arrive on the Other Side).

In busy urban emergency rooms people die surrounded by bright florescent lights, noise and chaos. In most ERs there are social workers present to counsel family members, but they're not trained to help the dying. In fact, nobody is the least bit interested in helping people die, because the ER is all about *preventing* death.

Dr. Neil Shocket, an emergency room physician at Kaiser Foundation Hospital in West Los Angeles, says, "There is an implied understanding that if you come to the ER, you want to be saved. So we focus on keeping people alive unless they have an advance directive[21] stating that no drastic measures will be taken to prolong life. We'll insert endotrachial tubes, put them on ventilators, re-start their hearts, inject chemicals, put invasive lines into their veins and never give up. It's what we were trained for. Keeping people alive is our default position.

"When we know the person can't be saved, we have to continue trying. If he is able to speak for himself, he can make the choice about whether to continue with life-saving interventions. If he's not able to speak for himself and the family is present, we'll ask the family to decide, but the family is completely unprepared for this. They've never discussed it or identified this scenario as a possibility, so they have a

---

[21] From www.FamilyDoctor.org: "An advance directive tells your doctor what kind of care you would like to have if you become unable to make medical decisions. A good advance directive describes the kind of treatment you would want depending on how sick you are. For example, the directives would describe what kind of care you want if you have an illness that you are unlikely to recover from, or if you are permanently unconscious. Advance directives usually tell your doctor that you don't want certain kinds of treatment. However, they can also say that you want a certain treatment no matter how ill you are. Laws about advance directives are different in each state."

terrible time making a decision. And even if a decision is made, the family members rarely agree with one another. It's a heartbreaking situation. I can't emphasize strongly enough how important it is for people to talk with their loved ones and make agreements about how they would like their deaths to be handled."

But how do we plan our exit strategies if nobody around us is willing to talk about it? On a personal note, my own father, who is 83 and sharp as a tack, flatly refuses to discuss death with me or my siblings. We have no idea how he feels about life support or whether he wants a formal religious funeral or a beach party. When asked, he cracks jokes and changes the subject. While this form of denial may provide some temporary comfort for *him*, it ultimately creates enormous difficulty for the entire family.

"In many ER cases, family members are not readily available, and this is particularly true for elderly nursing home patients whose next of kin live in another city or state," Dr. Shocket says. "Without a 'no code' or 'do not resuscitate' order, we'll keep the patient alive as long as possible. When the family is contacted, most of them have no idea what to do."

Those who have time to prepare for their deaths have excellent resources available from hospice services, and one of those resources is the opportunity to work with a trained professional who counsels the family on what to do when the patient has heart failure or stops breathing. For many hospice families, trips to the emergency room have become a way of life, but once the patient and his family accept the inevitability of death, the ER is no longer necessary. Hospice workers instruct families to call the hospice office instead of 911 when cardiac or respiratory failure occurs, but many families cannot bring themselves to do this, so 911 is called and the patient is resuscitated.

Allowing someone to die is not easy. It goes against all our natural survival instincts. In a perfect world, everybody would write an advance directive the moment they're born, but in reality, most people never do.

In a typical American emergency room, if the patient and/or his family has agreed to allow death to occur, there are rarely any resources available to help him make his transition. The social workers are busy counseling the family, the medical staff is busy keeping other people alive, the family is in shock, and nobody is there to skillfully assist the person in crossing the threshold. If there's time, the patient may request his own minister or rabbi, or a staff chaplain may be available for last rites, but very few modern clergy members are trained to assist with the process of dying.

Thankfully, there is a small but powerful movement underway in our culture dedicated to helping people understand and honor the sacred process of dying. Hospice workers, medical personnel, clergy, counselors and just plain folks now have many opportunities to learn how to act as effective "transition guides" or "death midwives" to help the dying move peacefully between worlds. While this idea is certainly not new in the west -- Catholic priests have been guiding people through the veil for centuries using the Ars Moriendi, a collection of texts created in the 15th century expressly for this purpose[22]-- it's almost unheard of in the modern age. The death midwifery movement is elegantly described by author and death midwife Rev. Joellyn St. Pierre:[23]

"The practice of Spiritual Death Midwifery is an art both ancient and new. It is a way of spiritually and energetically supporting one making the transition from this life into a new life with grace, dignity and deep reverence. It creates sacred space and offers the possibility that this most mysterious of life experiences be one of transformation and transcendence. Death Midwives act as guides and companions along this path we all will travel; a path that no one should be forced to travel alone.

"It is time to look closely at how we approach death in this culture. It is time to address not only the medical, but also the very important spiritual, emotional and energetic needs of the dying in an empathetic, artistic and intuitive way. Every birth experience is unique. Every death is as well. Both transitions are of the utmost importance and both are better served by the assistance of a compassionate and knowledgeable aide."

---

[22] http://www.deathreference.com/A-Bi/Ars-Moriendi.html
[23] http://deathmidwifery.com

A caregiver, family member or trained transition coach can work with the dying person by simply sitting beside him and reading from his favorite spiritual texts or poetry. She might talk to him about the beautiful journey he's about to take, and describe whatever imagery he finds comforting, be it angels, ancestors or a beloved pet waiting to greet him. She might play his favorite music, or talk to him about the beauty and value of his life, assuring him that he is loved and safe. Often, if there's time and if the patient is able, a coach will work with the family to heal rifts, express love or share forgiveness.

Transition coach Diane Goble, in her book, *Beginner's Guide to Conscious Dying*, outlines specific techniques for conscious dying, including practicing to die *before* we die via the use of guided meditations and imagery. Goble says:

"A life threatening diagnosis is a wake-up call to include the practice of conscious dying in your overall treatment plan. Meditation and guided imagery, with the help of a trained Transition Guide, can be used for *practicing* to die before we die.

"Most of us aren't prepared for our return to the spiritual world. Our first reaction may be fear and resistance to what's happening, and we may try to go back to what is familiar to us. This is why it's important to have someone guide us through the various stages and assure us that we will not have to face wrath or judgment. When dying is considered an integral part of life, essential to one's spiritual growth and conscious evolution, people are free to be more open with their feelings and compassionate in their caring. They are able to express their feelings and beliefs about death, dying, and the afterlife. The dying are able to put their lives in perspective and the family is able to be supportive. With the shared realization that we don't die, we simply grow and move on to the next developmental stage of life, we are all able to help each other deal with our shared loss and grief over the *temporary* separation caused by the death of the body."

For every dying person or grieving family that anticipates an endless dark void or a fiery hell, there's another that looks forward to being gently carried into the light by loving guides from another dimension. Regardless of the circumstances, whether we're dying peacefully in our beds or in the chaos of an emergency room or an accident scene, at some point in the dying process, we are eager and ready to return home. Diane Goble explains:

"In the early twilight stage, we experience consciousness in two dimensions simultaneously. We drift back and forth from the physical dimension to the spiritual dimension, letting go of one, adjusting to the other, as if we have become a bubble, floating effortlessly, directed by our thoughts. Our awareness of what *is* expands beyond the limits of our physical senses, and we begin remembering all that we had forgotten. We may be having a conversation with our loved ones on the Other Side and then drift back to our bed where our loved ones on this side are relieved to see us lucid again. They think we've been unconscious. We don't notice there is a difference because it is all happening in the moment. Those on this side may assume we are hallucinating, but we are communicating with those on the Other Side, because in our awareness, there is no *other* side."

THE HEALING POWER OF RITUAL

In order to fully process grief, trauma or transition of any kind, ritual is a mandatory step in the journey to healing. There are other valuable resources of course, including counseling, meditation, support groups, books and spiritual practice, but without ritual, these other tools only get the job partially done.

Ritual gives words to the unspeakable and form to the formless. It brings the non-physical into physical form so we can see it, touch it, feel it and process it. Creating this link between Heaven and Earth helps us to see the connection clearly, and to establish a bond between the realms, which gives us great comfort. It brings the spirit of the dead person into the body of the grieving person, and closes the perceived gap between them.

In my work as an author, teacher and grief guidance facilitator, I've been asked many times to suggest simple rituals that can help with the process of facing and walking through painful changes, particularly the death of a loved one. Some of the rituals described here involve the participation of the person who is dying, and some are exclusively for those who remain on earth. These rituals presume that an honest dialog about death has already begun.

Create a Journey Blanket

If you have a loved one who is dying, consider creating a memorial quilt or "journey blanket" for him or her. 18 months before my son died, I gathered a group of friends in my living room for a potluck dinner and a quilting bee. Each person brought a piece of fabric that had special meaning to them, and these -- along with pieces of fabric from Danny's own life -- were cobbled into a beautiful patchwork quilt, filled with love, prayers and blessings. It was far from technically perfect, with sloppy stitching and uneven squares, but the energy it held was magical. The quilt was very warm and Danny slept with it for the next two winters. The following summer he died lying on top of that quilt, and now I sleep and meditate with it, and it has become *my* journey blanket also.

Get a Tattoo

Many of the firefighters who battled the blaze at the World Trade Center on September 11, 2001 felt unbearable grief and guilt about the partners who'd fought beside them and perished. Some of them processed and ritualized their grief by having images of their fallen friends tattooed on their backs. The firefighters said, "This way I will have my partner's spirit with me every day of my life." When I heard about this, I asked Danny (11 years old at the time) what animal he would be if he could choose to be one. He chose a swan, and the following week I had a tattoo of a swan on my left shoulder.

Locks of Love

In the days leading up to Danny's death, while he was in and out of consciousness, I often sat beside him stroking his beautiful, thick hair. One day I realized that locks of his hair would make extraordinary gifts for the people who loved him, so with his permission, I snipped small pieces and tied each with a delicate red ribbon. I've given them all away except for the one I kept for myself.

Put it in a Locket

I keep a tiny snippet of that hair in a heart-shaped locket that I wear almost every day.

Open the Treasure Chest and Give the Riches Away

When you're ready to start going through your departed loved one's possessions, think of it as a sacred rite of passage. Invite friends to help, and light candles, say prayers, open a bottle of champagne (or several bottles) and share memories, stories, laughter and tears as you look through the precious objects. Set aside selected items to give to friends as remembrance tokens, or make something wonderful and creative out of them. One of my friends had a quilt made from her husband's favorite shirts, and another made pillowcases from her mother's antique tablecloths.

Hold Court

If the dying person is open to it and is physically capable, he can choose which belongings he'd like to give to friends and family members. When my friend Betty was dying, she asked her sons to display her special possessions around the house. She was a collector of healing crystals, and the dining room table was covered with magnificent geodes, quartz obelisks, rare stones and other sacred objects. Her friends were invited to take whatever pieces called out to them, with Betty's full participation and blessing. She even chose to have her memorial service while she was still alive. Friends gathered at her house to tell heartwarming stories about their experiences with Betty, light candles, sing songs and recite beautiful prayers and readings while Betty sat up in her bed, beaming with happiness.

Plant a Tree or a Memorial Garden

If you can't plant a tree or shrub in a public place in honor of your loved one, create a special corner of your yard as a memorial garden.

Plant special trees and flowers there, and decorate the space with pictures, sacred objects, religious icons or anything that inspires you. If your loved one was cremated, this is an excellent place to sprinkle some of the ashes. The students at Danny''s high school raised money to purchase a magnolia tree, which was planted in his honor in front of the special education building where he'd spent the last year of his academic life.

Send your Loved One on a World Tour

There are many creative and meaningful ways to use cremation ashes (also known as "cremains") in ceremony, and the ceremonies do not have to be formal or somber. Because Danny loved to travel, I divided some of his ashes into tiny, decorated bottles and gave one to each of our closest friends to carry with them on their vacations and business trips. His ashes have now been sprinkled in at least a dozen countries. We're aiming for all seven continents eventually.

Keep Your Loved One's Name Alive

Four months after Danny died I had my last name legally changed to his first name... Daniel. You may not want to go so far as to legally change your name, but you can find dozens of imaginative ways to keep your loved one's name alive. Use her nickname as one of your computer passwords, or start a business, charitable group or website using a variation of it. Engrave his name on a paving stone for your memorial garden, or hire a graphic artist to design a logo or icon for the name.

Recommended Reading

DEATH AND DYING

An American Book of Dying - Richard Groves
Final Exit - Derek Humphries
Final Gifts - Maggie Callanan and Patricia Kelley
Who Dies? Stephen Levine
On Death and Dying - Elizabeth Kubler-Ross
The Art of Death Midwifery - Rev. Joellyn St. Pierre
Dying Well - Ira Byock
Beginner's Guide to Conscious Dying - Diane Goble

INNER WORK , MEDITATION, THE JOURNEY OF THE SOUL

A Course in Miracles - Helen Schucman and William Thetford
Conversations With God – Neale Donald Walsch
Grist for the Mill - Ram Dass
Love Without End: Jesus Speaks – Glenda Green
Personal Growth Through Awareness – Sanaya Roman
Entering the Castle - by Caroline Myss
Spiritual Growth – Sanaya Roman
Start Where You Are - Pema Chodron
The Disappearance of the Universe – Gary Renard
The Nature of Personal Reality - Jane Roberts/Seth
The Only Dance There is - Ram Dass
The Places That Scare You - Pema Chodron
When Things Fall Apart - Pema Chodron
A Swan in Heaven - Terri Daniel
The Teachings of Abraham - Esther and Jerry Hicks
Emmanuel's Book - Pat Rodegast and Judith Stanton

CHANNELING

Opening to Channel – Sanaya Roman, Duane Packer
Messages From Angels - Doreen Virtue
Contacting Your Spirit Guide - Sylvia Browne

LIFE AFTER DEATH, AFTERLIFE , REINCARNATION

Home With God in a Life That Never Ends -- Neale Donald Walsch
After Life - John Edward
Animals on the Other Side - Sylvia Brown
Blessings from the Other Side – Sylvia Browne
Children's Past Lives - Carol Bowman
Life After Life - Raymond Moody
Talking to Heaven - James Van Praagh
The Other Side and Beyond – Sylvia Browne
There is No Death - Betty Bethards
Tibetan Book of the Dead

OUT OF BODY EXPERIENCE

Journeys out of the Body - Robert Monroe
The Third Eye - Tuesday Lopsang Rampa
Astral Projection Techniques - Sylvia Browne
Far Journeys – Robert Monroe

PSYCHIC DEVELOPMENT

Second Sight - Judith Orloff
Awakening the Second Sight - Judith Orloff
My Psychic Journey - Chris Dufresne

THE SHAMAN'S VIEW

Journey to Ixtlan - Carlos Castaneda
Tales of Power - Carlos Castaneda
Teachings of Don Juan - Carlos Castaneda
The Four Agreements - Manuel Ruiz

PRE-CHRISTIAN HISTORY, RELIGION/MYTHOLOGY

The Mists of Avalon - Marion Zimmer Bradley
Pagan Ways - Gwydion O'Hara
The Power of Myth - Joseph Campbell
A Pagan Book of Living and Dying - Starhawk

CHRISTIANITY/BIBLE

The Other Bible - W. Barnstone
Love Without End: Jesus Speaks - Glenda Green
The Dark Side of Christian History - Helen Ellerbe
The Christian Myth - Burton Mack
Who Wrote the New Testament - Burton Mack
Misquoting Jesus - Bart Ehrman
Jesus, Interrupted - Bart Ehrman
The Gnostic Gospels - Elaine Pagels
The Good Book - David Plotz

ENERGETIC HEALING

Anatomy of the Spirit by Caroline Myss
Healing and Sprituality - Joan Z. Borysenko
Healing With Spirit - Carolyn Myss
Karma Releasing - Doreen Virtue
The Lightworker's Way - Doreen Virtue
You Can Heal Your Life - Louise Hay

Conscious Dying and Afterlife Resources

Zen Hospice Project
www.zenhospice.org
415.863.2910   mail@zenhospice.org

Yumtha Center
for Conscious Living and Dying
www.yumtha.org
707-829-6893   yumtha@msn.com

The Sacred Art of Living Center
(The Anamcara Project)
www.sacredartofliving.org
888-383-4171   info@sacredartofliving.org

National Hospice and
Palliative Care Association
www.nhpco.org
800/658-8898   consumers@nhpco.org.

Final Passages
Green and Loving Family-Directed Home Funerals
www.finalpassages.org
(707) 824-0268   info@finalpassages.org

Beyond the Veil
Transition Guide Training
www.beyondtheveil.net
310.489.0862   transitionguide@mac.com

Living/Dying Project
www.livingdying.org
(415) 456-3915   info@livingdying.org

International Assn. of Near Death Studies (IANDS)
www.iands.org
(919) 383-7940   info@iands.org

After Death Communication
Research Foundation
(ADCRF) adcrf@adcrf.org

The Friday Afterlife Report
An Excellent Weekly Newsletter About Afterlife Topics
www.VictorZammit.com

The ADC Project
Dedicated to After-Death Communication (ADC)
www.after-death.com

The Afterlife Education Foundation
www.AfterlifeConference.com

Please visit our
Afterlife Awareness
Facebook page!

Our website:
www.AfterlifeAwareness.com

About the Authors

Terri Daniel is a spiritual teacher, hospice worker and Certified Transition Guide who works with assistance from the Other Side to advance a metaphysical perspective on birth, death and the afterlife. Her previous book, *A Swan In Heaven,* is based on after-death dialogs between Terri and her son Danny, who left the physical plane in 2006.

Terri conducts workshops and metaphysical study groups, and also counsels bereaved individuals by offering alternative perspectives on the grief experience. She has spoken on the topic of conscious death to community gatherings, churches, bereavement groups, hospices and spiritual conferences, and her articles have been published in Whole Life Times, Neurology Today, Exceptional Parent, Pure Inspiration, Special Child, Children's Hospice.org and related websites.

Danny Snowden-Mandell was born in 1990. As a healthy, happy young boy, Danny loved swimming, skiing, fighter jets, Lego models, James Bond and The Simpsons. He excelled at reading, storytelling and video games.

Danny died at age 16 from a rare disease called *Metachromatic Leukodystropy*, and immediately began communicating with his mother from the Other Side. Along with his guides and teachers in Heaven, Danny works through Terri to assist her in bringing his message to spiritual seekers on earth, especially those who are struggling with loss and grief.

LaVergne, TN USA
16 December 2010
209032LV00002B/1/P